Warwick Goble's Fairy Tales:
A Vintage Grayscale Adult Coloring Book

By Ligia Ortega
ColoringPress.com

This book is dedicated to my dear friend Karen. Thank you for caring, listening, offering advice, encouragement, and for all the kindness you give. I am so grateful to have you in my life.

Artist's Message

It means so much that you have chosen to purchase this book. I hope it brings you or a loved one hours of coloring pleasure.

All images in this book were lovingly sourced, curated, and restored by me. I then worked to carefully convert every image to high-quality colorable grayscale, digitize every page and assemble them electronically to prepare for printing. This coloring book has been a true labor of love, representing months of work (plus sleep deprivation and neglect of friendships and housework!). Although the source images are public domain, the work I have done to restore and convert these images into grayscale coloring pages is protected by Copyright Law. I took the time and additional expense to officially register this book with the Copyright Office. Please respect Copyright Law.

You may:

Copy the uncolored pages on other paper preferences for yourself.
Post colored images on social media.
Give the colored pages as gifts.
Give a physical book you purchased as a gift.

You may not:

Share physical or electronic copies of uncolored pages with anyone else, whether free or for sale.
Post uncolored pages anywhere online, claim them as your own, or distribute uncolored pages via e-mail or electronic downloads.
Incorporate uncolored or colored images on items besides colored pages.
Sell uncolored or colored images, cards, or crafts made with the coloring pages, use them on products, or for any commercial usage.

Copyright © 2017 Ligia Ortega. All rights reserved. I am grateful for your support of artist/author's rights.

In accordance with the U.S. Copyright Act of 1976, the scanning, uploading, and electronic sharing of any part of this book without the permission of the artist/author constitutes unlawful **piracy** and **theft** of the artist/author's intellectual property except for the provisions above. Coloring any image does not transfer copyright or any rights to you, nor does it create a new copyright in your name. If you would like to use material from the book, prior written permission must be obtained by contacting the artist/author at:

ColoringGifts@yahoo.com   ColoringPress.com   www.facebook.com/ColoringPress

ISBN: 978-1976137235

ISBN: 1976137233

THIS BOOK BELONGS TO:

_____

About This Book

Early in my art career I was exposed to the work of several turn-of-the-century illustrators, and I discovered a few favorites whose work I spent hours poring over. One of these illustrators was Warwick Goble. This all happened in the days before the internet, so finding work by these artists took some dedicated searching. The local library didn't have anything and I finally found myself digging around the stacks of the local university's fine arts library, giddy to find books of his work. I was delighted a few years later when I enrolled and was finally able to get a library card for the university's library because it meant I could actually bring some of these books home with me instead of spending hours at library stacks looking at illustrations.

While working on other adult coloring books, I remembered Warwick Goble's work, and thought wouldn't it be wonderful to take the exquisite work done by this amazing illustrator and introduce it to a whole new generation of people? I got to work and began researching, sourcing illustrations, curating them to the best ones, and spent hours sorting them into several collections. Then the real work began. These illustrations could not be separated from his original technique and rather than being converted to line art, the best way to maintain the integrity of these works would be to let them have the nuances of grayscale. I worked to restore the illustrations (the originals I was able to source were made approximately 100 years ago, so they needed hours of work to be made into this finished book) and then finally digitizing the images to get them ready to print. I researched and learned how to make the best possible colorable grayscale page (it's a lot more complex than simply making an image black and white) and after converting the restored, digitized illustrations to grayscale, set out to assemble the images into this book. This is the second book in a series, and I will be working on more vintage grayscale adult coloring books showcasing several of my favorite vintage artists and illustrators.

Warwick Goble (1862-1943) was a British illustrator of children's books. Like many artists of his time he was influenced by Japanese woodblock prints and also had visible influence from East Indian art. His illustrations are a beautiful combination of line and color and tend to have an exotic flair to them.

I am already working on the next volume of my vintage grayscale adult coloring book series. Please visit my site at ColoringPress.com or find me on Facebook at facebook.com/ColoringPress to share your colored pages, to get grayscale coloring tips, and for more information on my next volumes in this series.

Thank you for choosing this volume and I hope you enjoy coloring Warwick Goble's delightful work!

Ligia Ortega

Illustrations

Listed in order of appearance

The Fairy Book

- A beautiful young girl lay asleep
- After care of Fairy Tulip she was not wounded
- Are you not sometimes called Rumpelstilzchen
- At even-tide she climbed into a tree
- At last she remembered her dream
- Avenant delivered up his phial
- Give me a sack and a pair of boots
- He flew in and perched on her shoulder
- He led the trembling Aslog over the snow
- Her name was Snowdrop
- Hop-o-my-thumb
- I know not of any happiness I could wish for
- Is it far from hence asked the wolf
- Jack reached the top of the beanstalk
- Laid in a cradle of mother-of-pearl
- Out of the fire flew a beautiful bird
- Riquet with the Tuft appeared in her eyes
- She climbed up and broke off a branch
- She gave the handkerchief to the magician
- She let her hair fall loose
- Surprised by the appearance of a mermaid
- The beasts of prey turned into three lambs
- The butterfly took wing
- The cock crowed for the third time
- The eagle let his prey go
- The fairy there welcome her majesty
- The king took the maiden on his own horse
- The king's daughter was overjoyed
- The lady then gave him a purse
- The only remnants being the glass slippers
- The queen threw her shirt over them
- They turned into bundles of feathers

The Book of Fairy Poetry

- And I should look like a fountain of gold
- Down to the rocks where the serpents creep
- Nautilus is my boat
- Sea-nymphs hourly ring his knell
- What form she pleased each thing would take

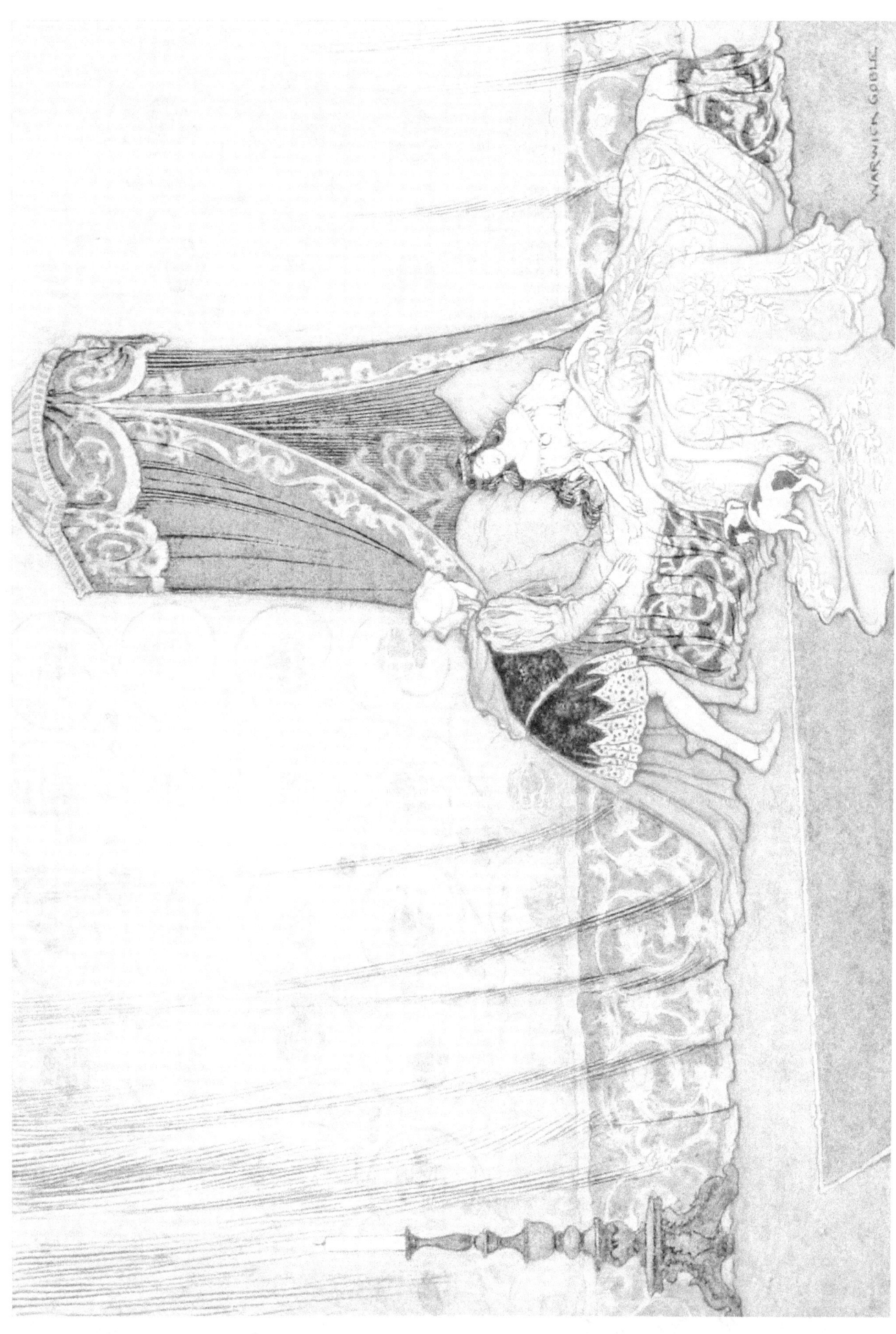

Warwick Goble's Fairy Tales © Ligia Ortega - ColoringPress.com

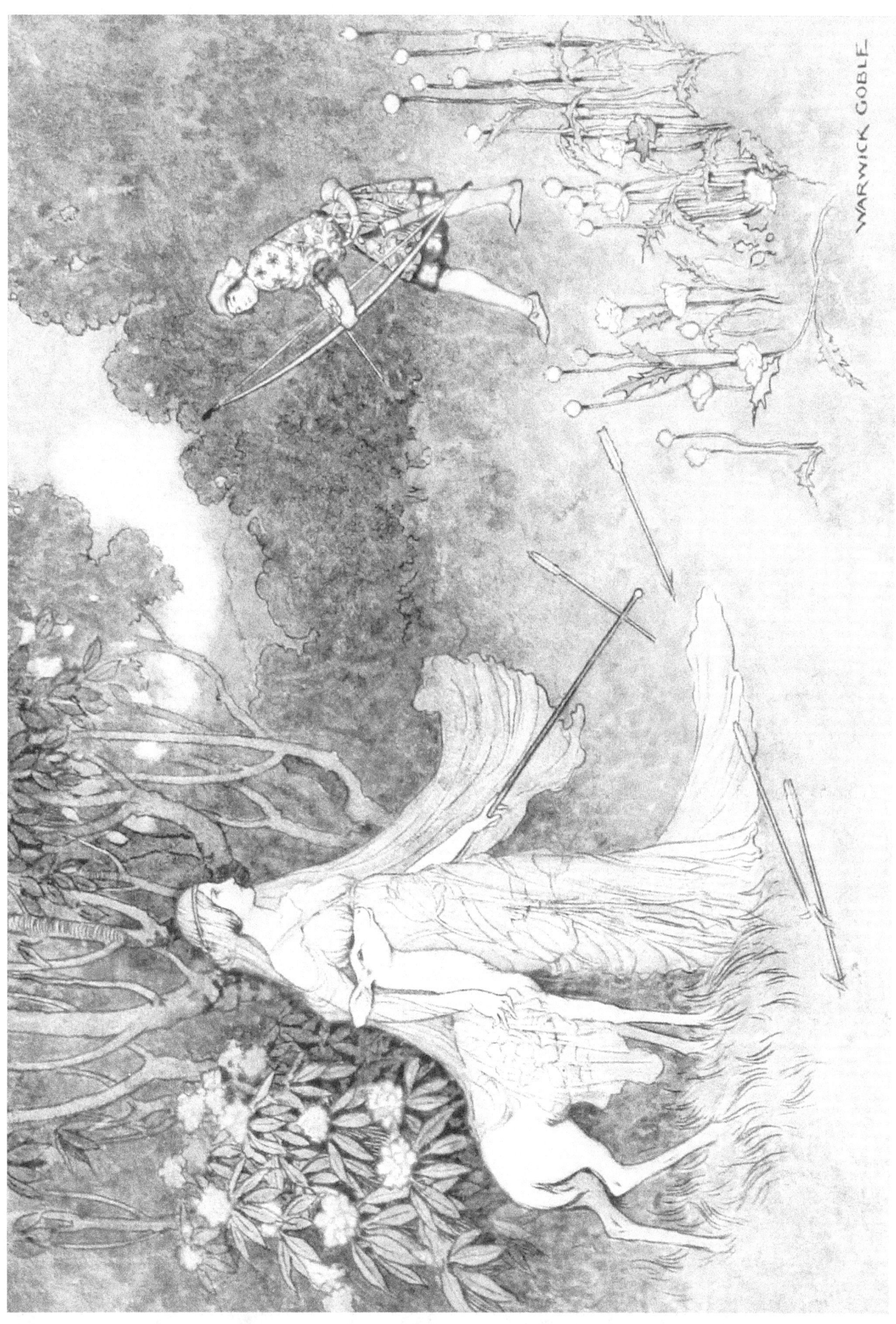

Warwick Goble's Fairy Tales

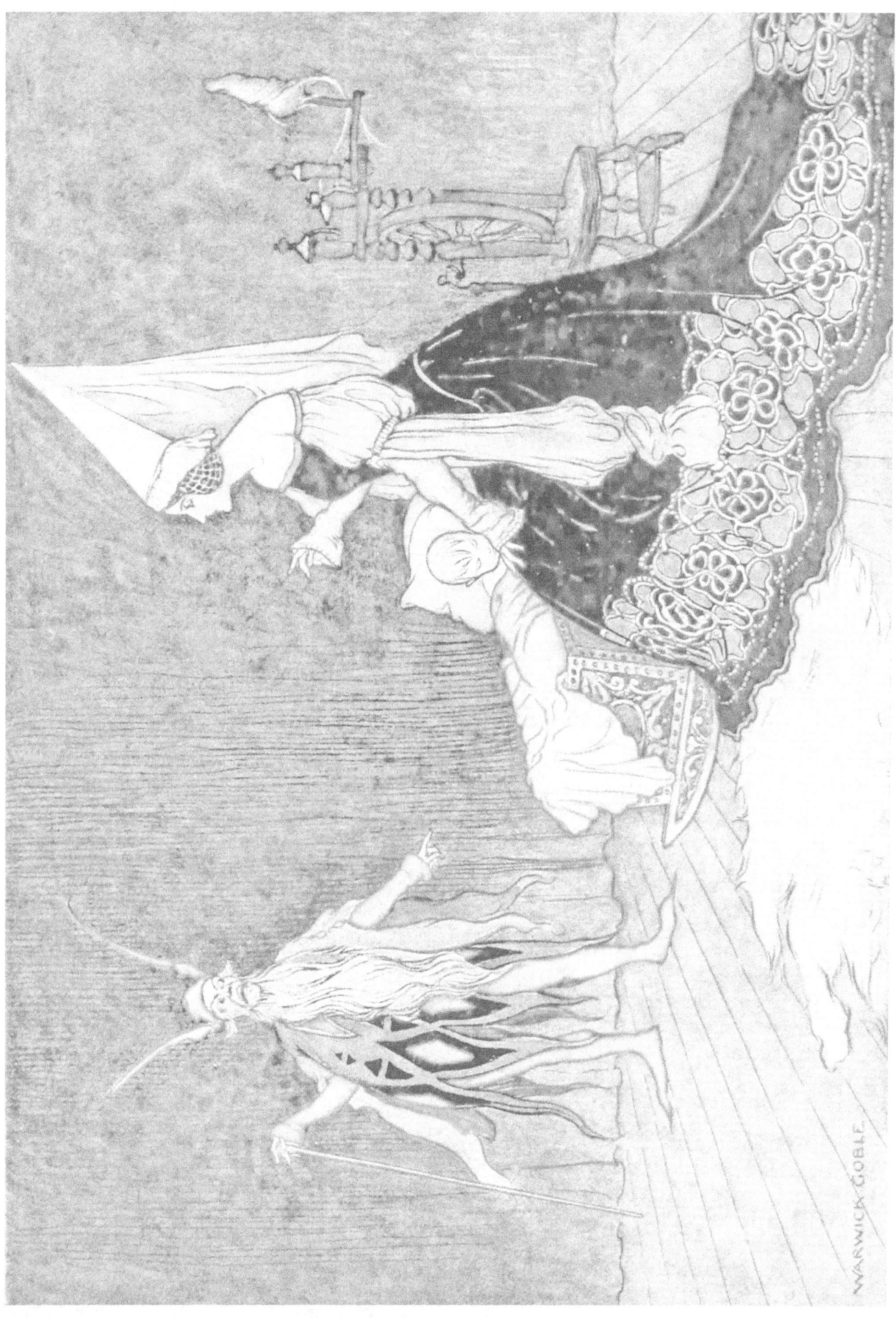

Warwick Goble's Fairy Tales

© Ligia Ortega - ColoringPress.com

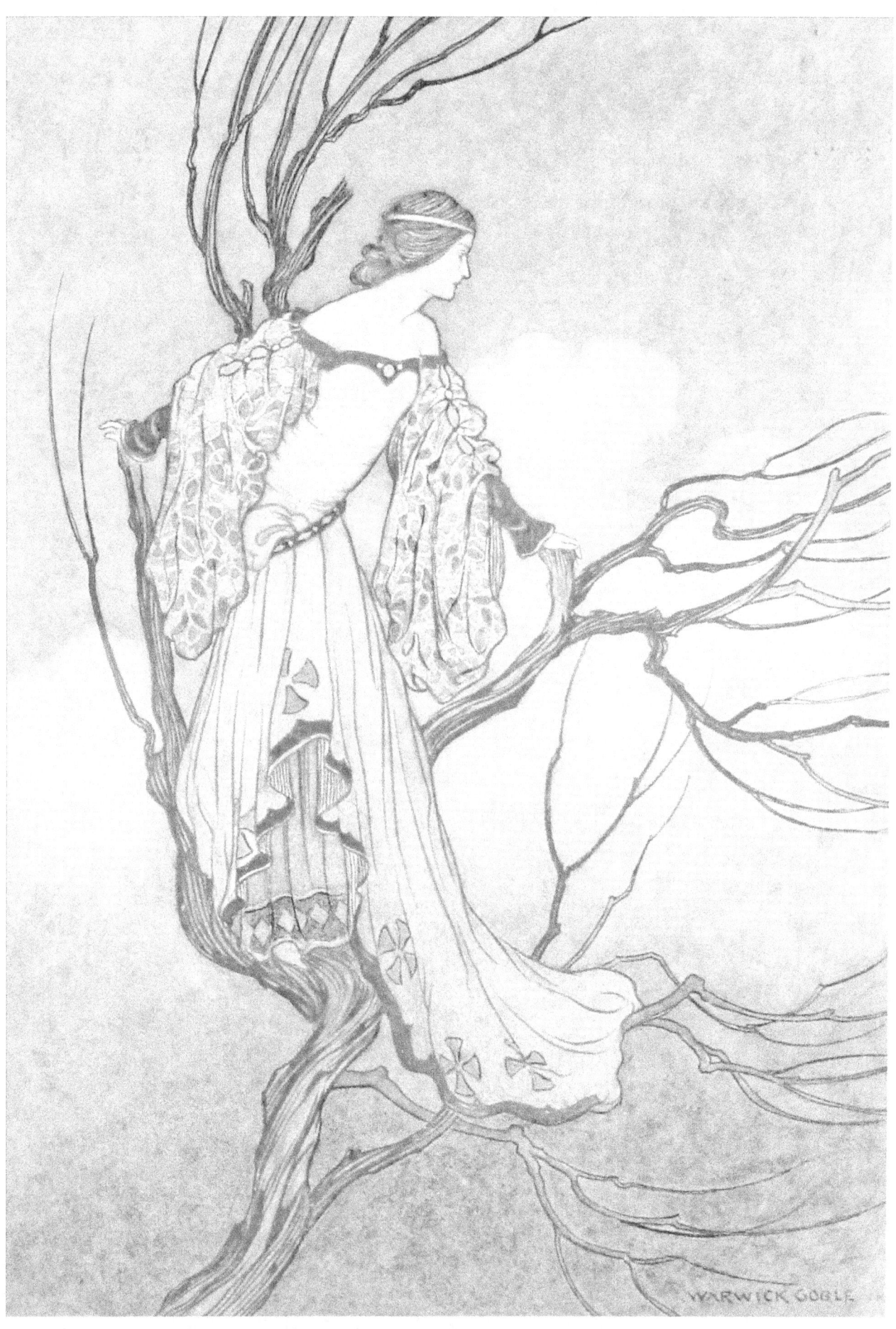

Warwick Goble's Fairy Tales © Ligia Ortega - ColoringPress.com

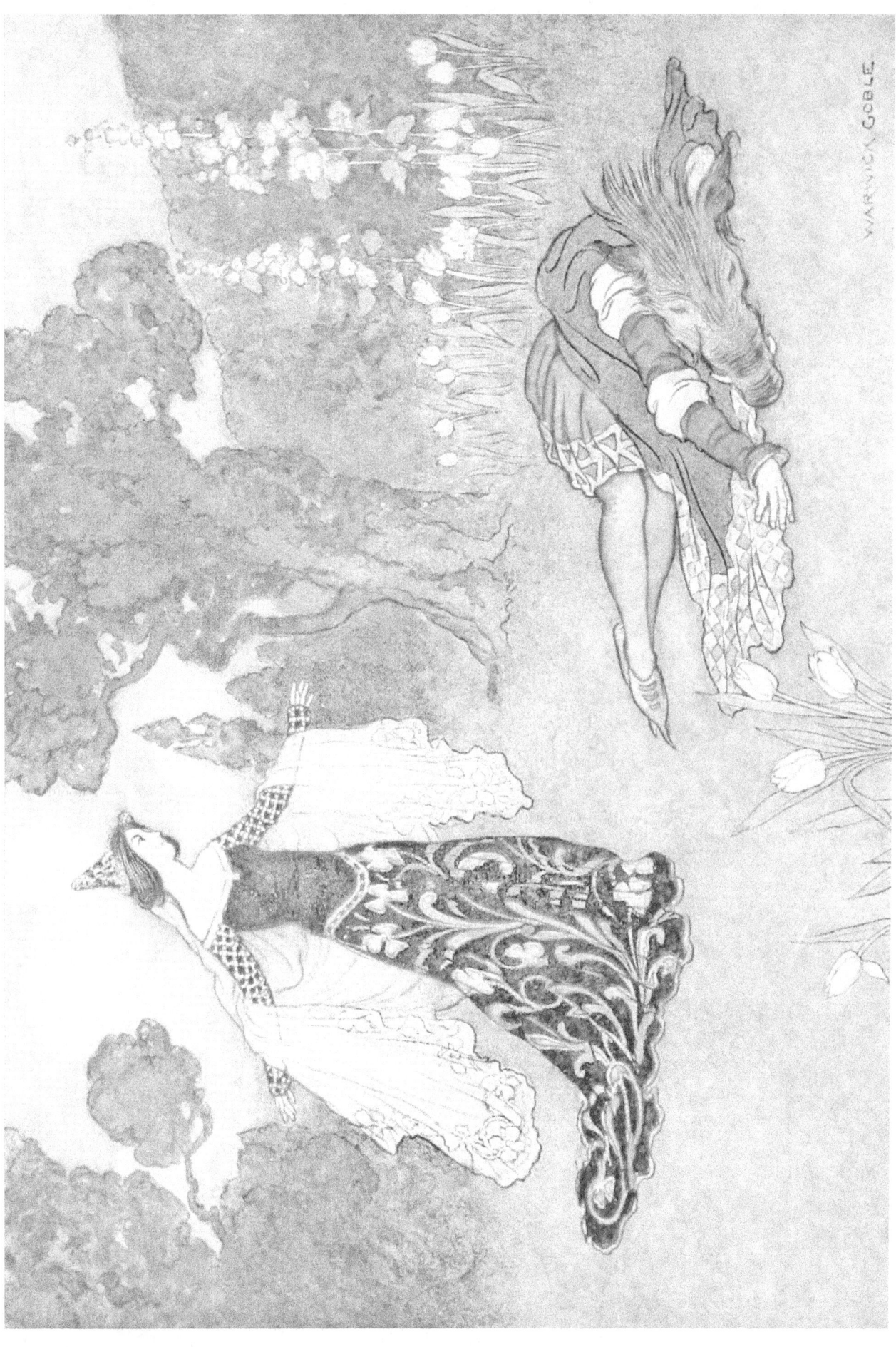

Warwick Goble's Fairy Tales

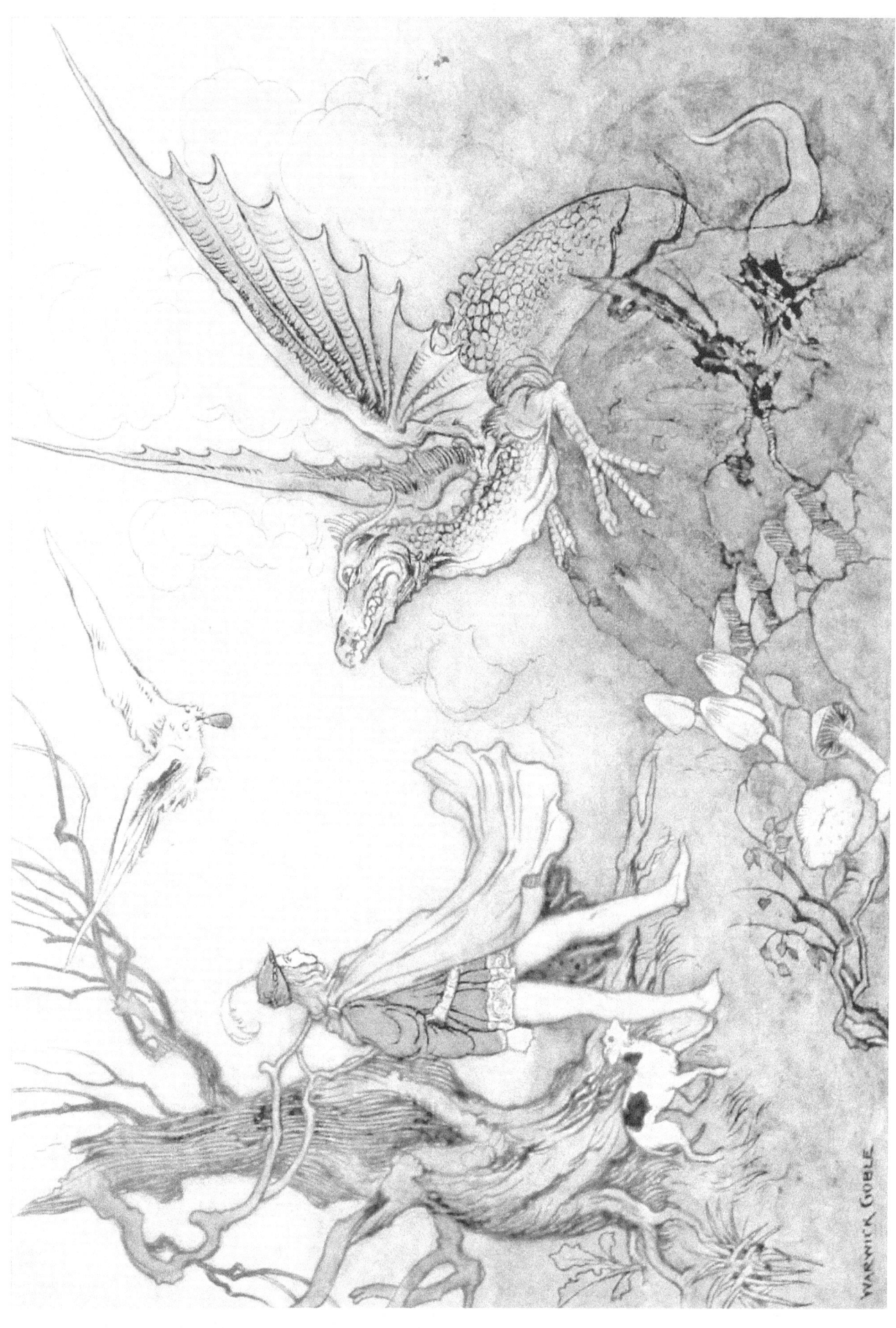

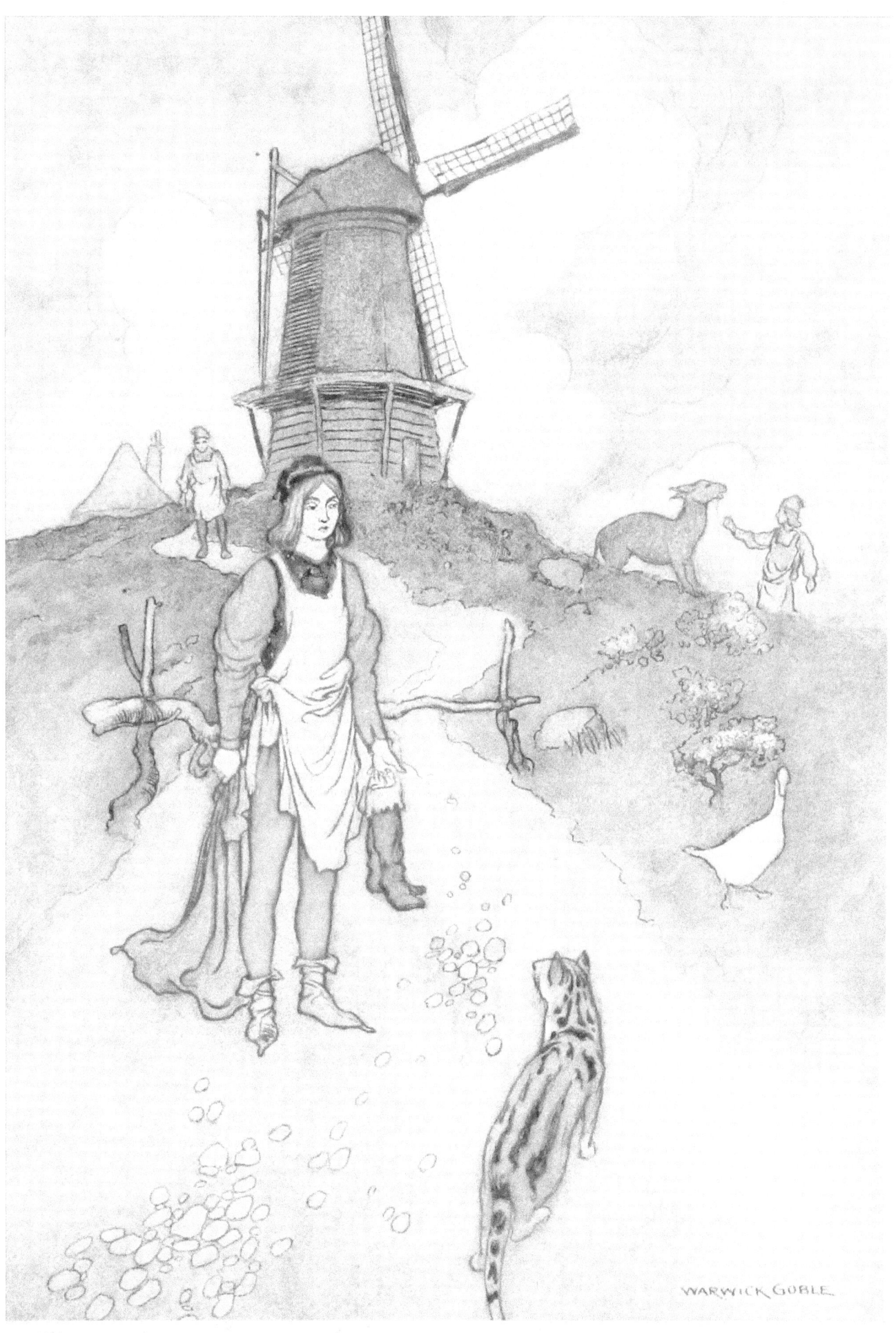

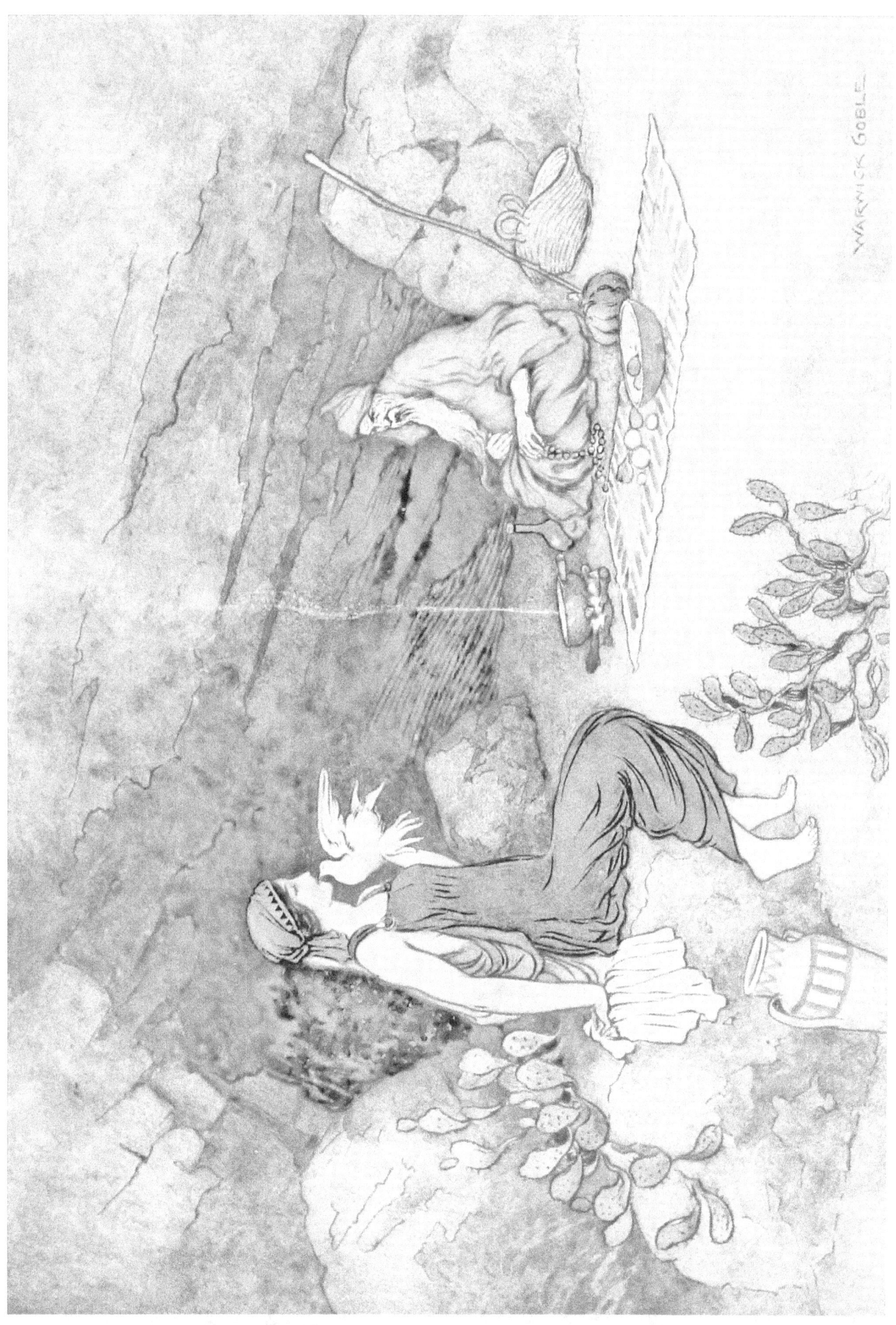

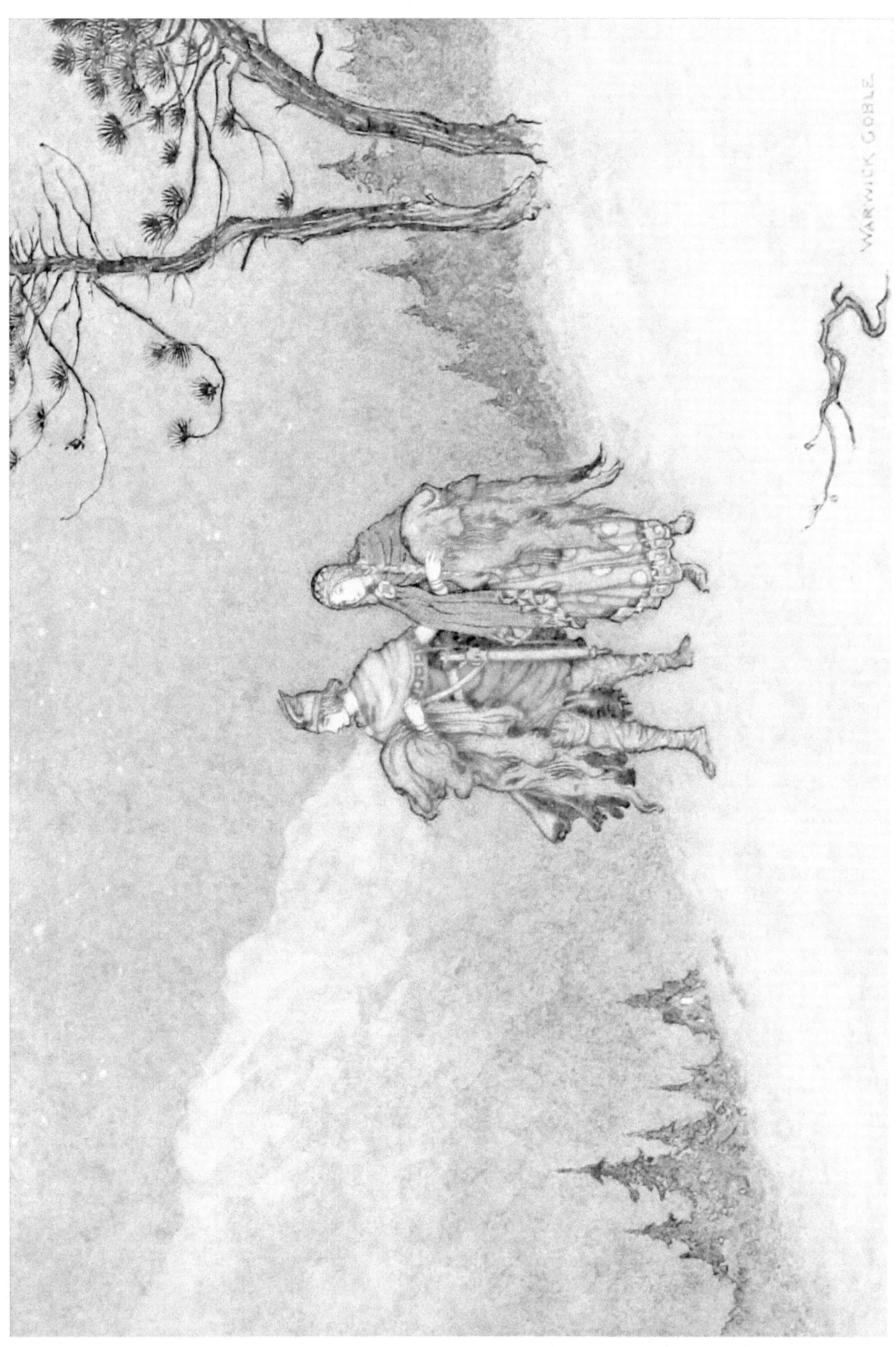

Warwick Goble's Fairy Tales

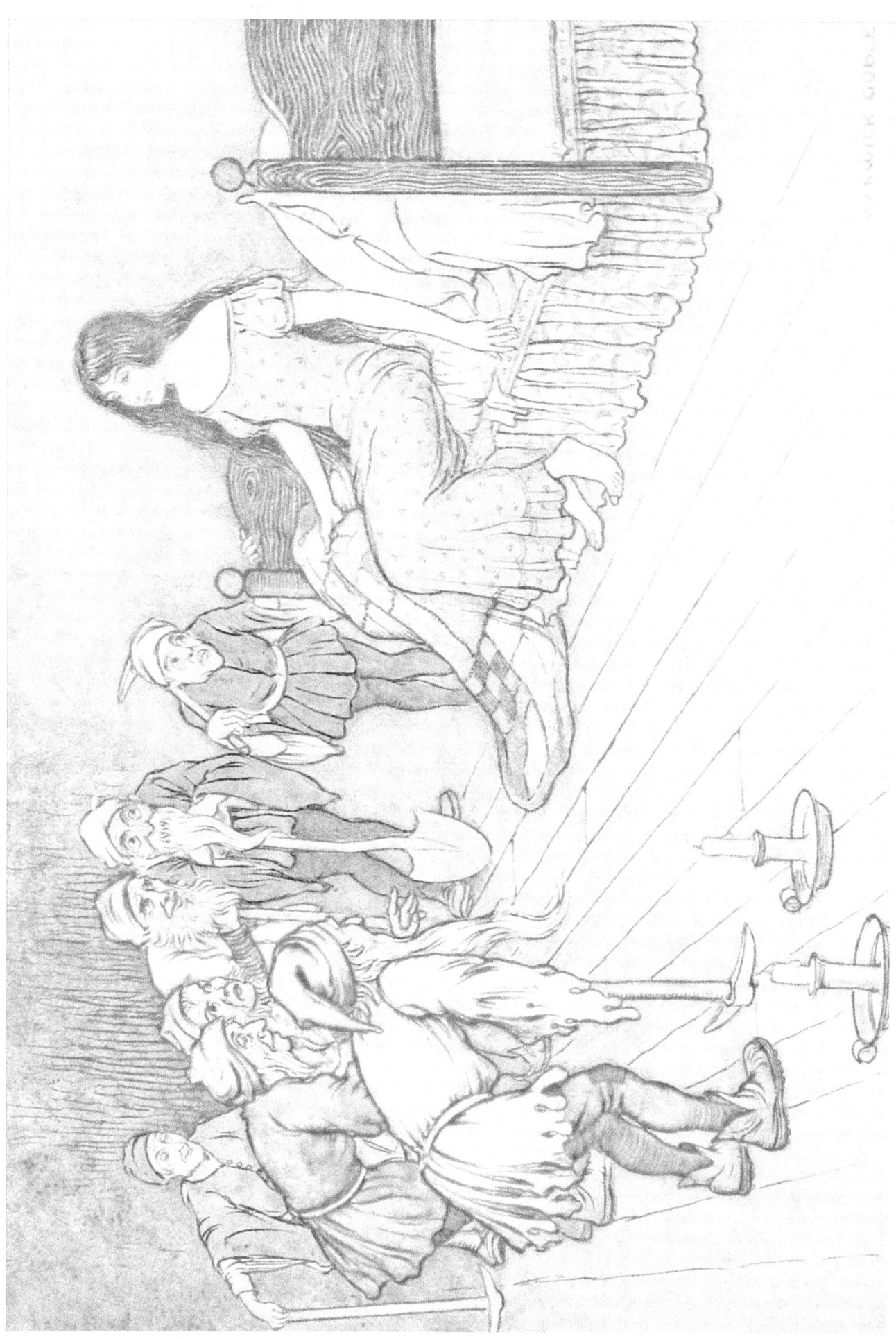

Warwick Goble's Fairy Tales

© Ligia Ortega - ColoringPress.com

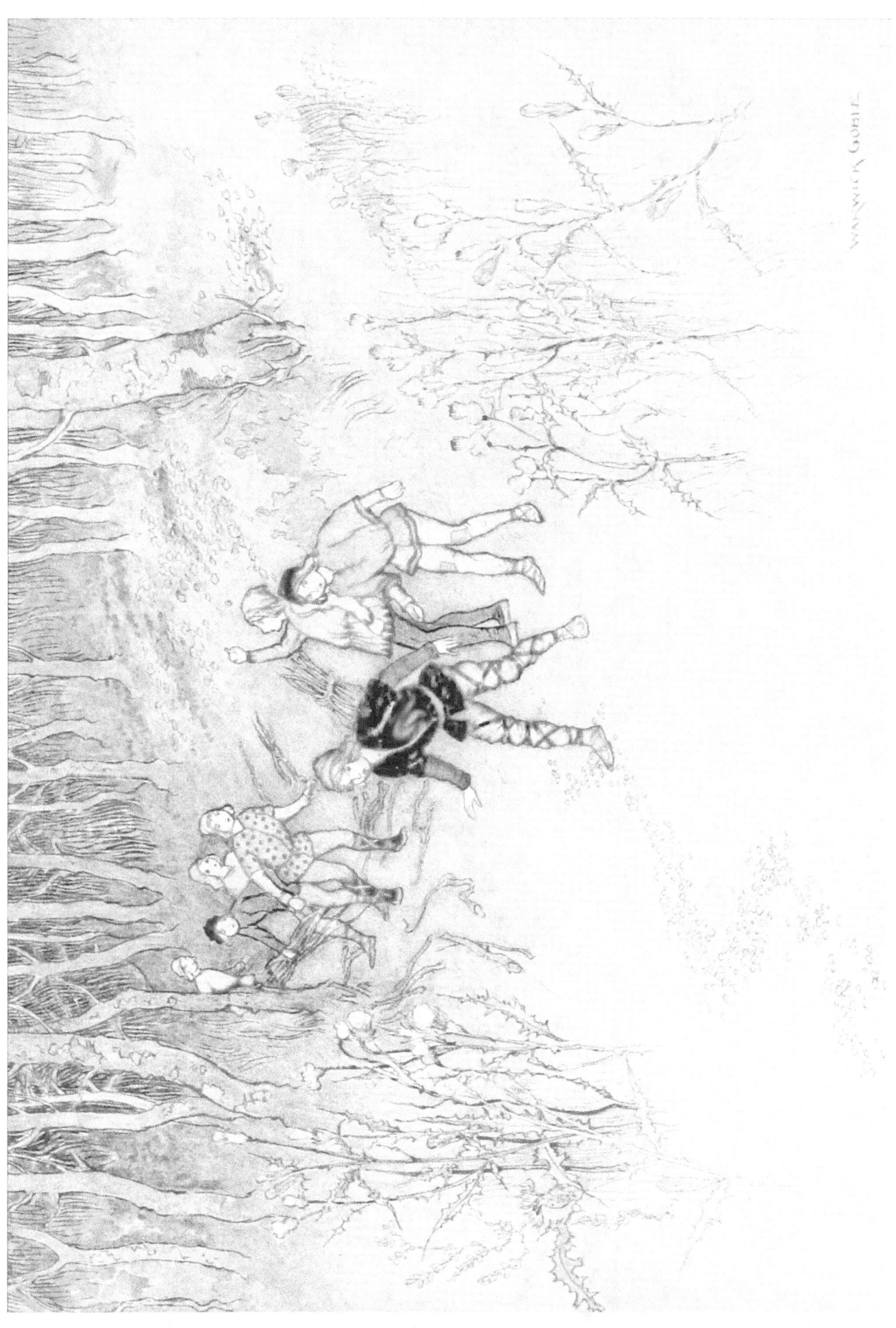

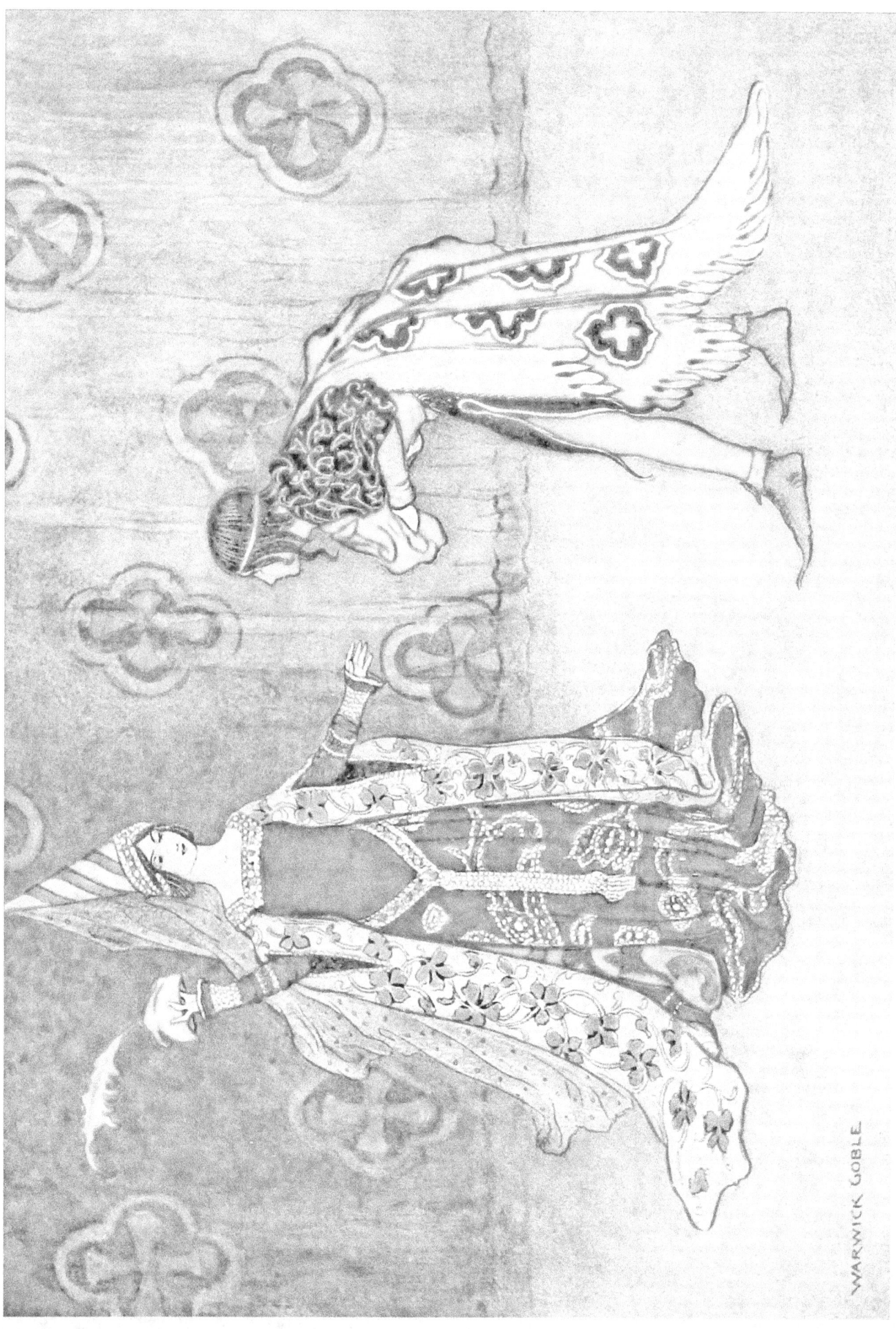

Warwick Goble's Fairy Tales

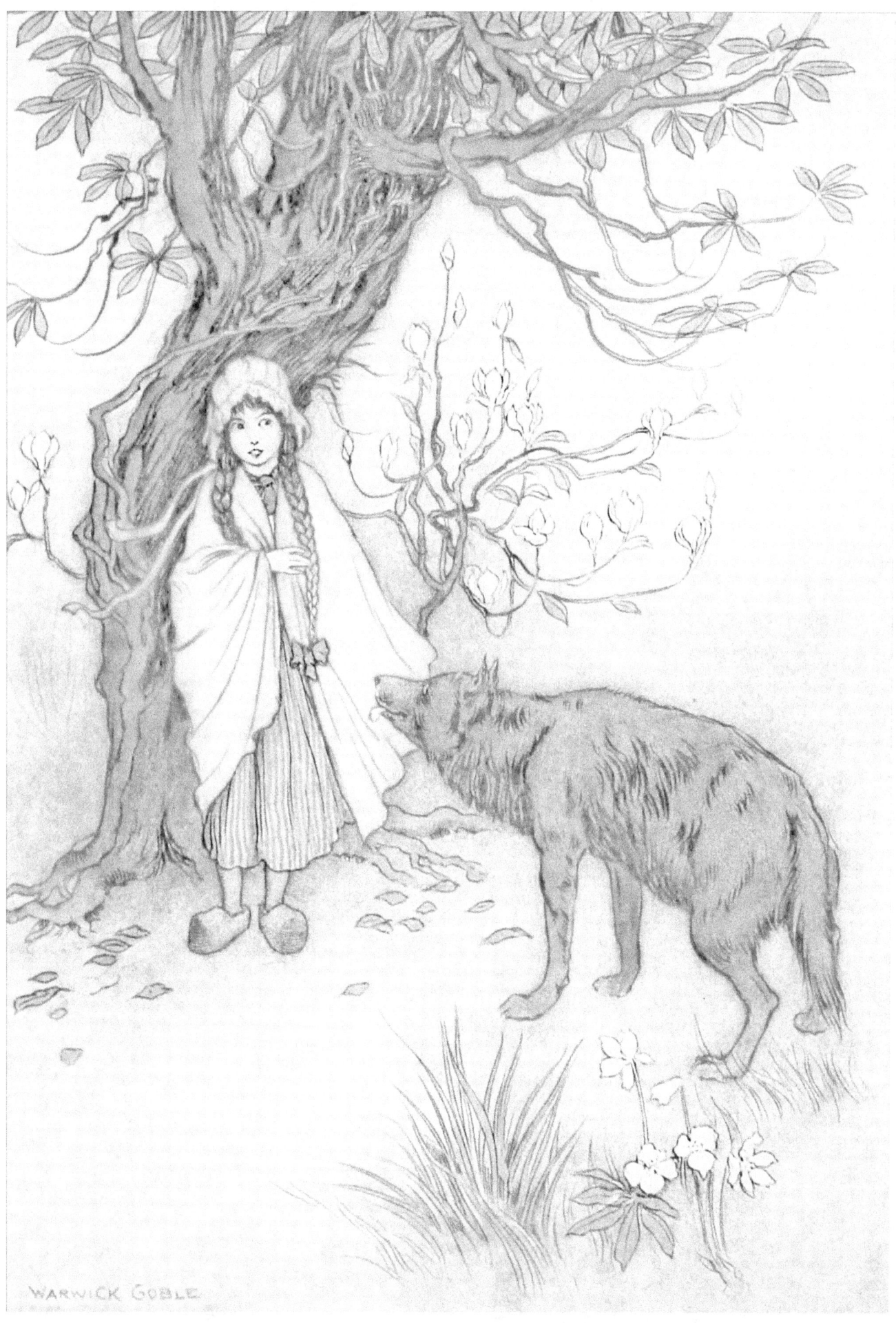

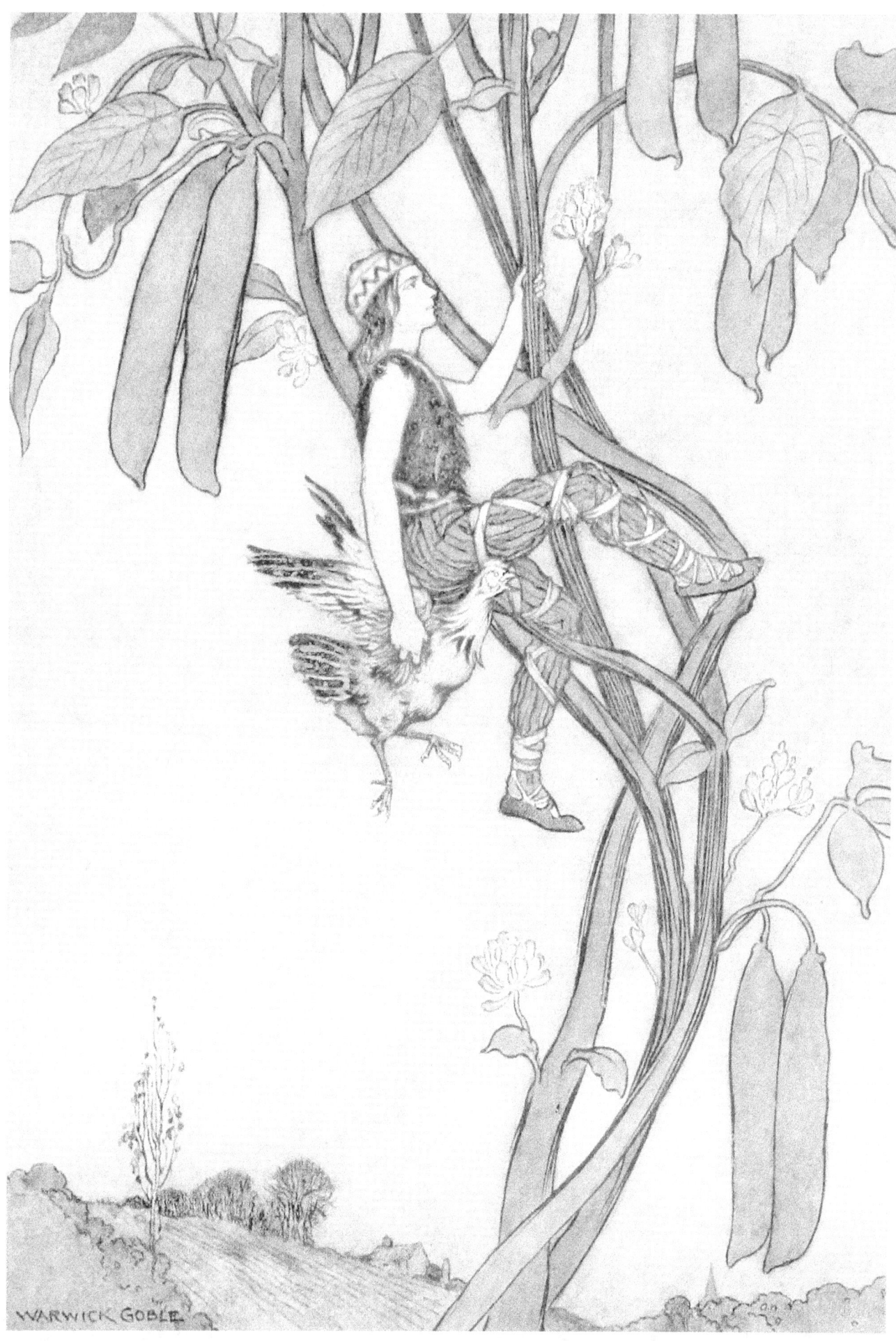

Warwick Goble's Fairy Tales

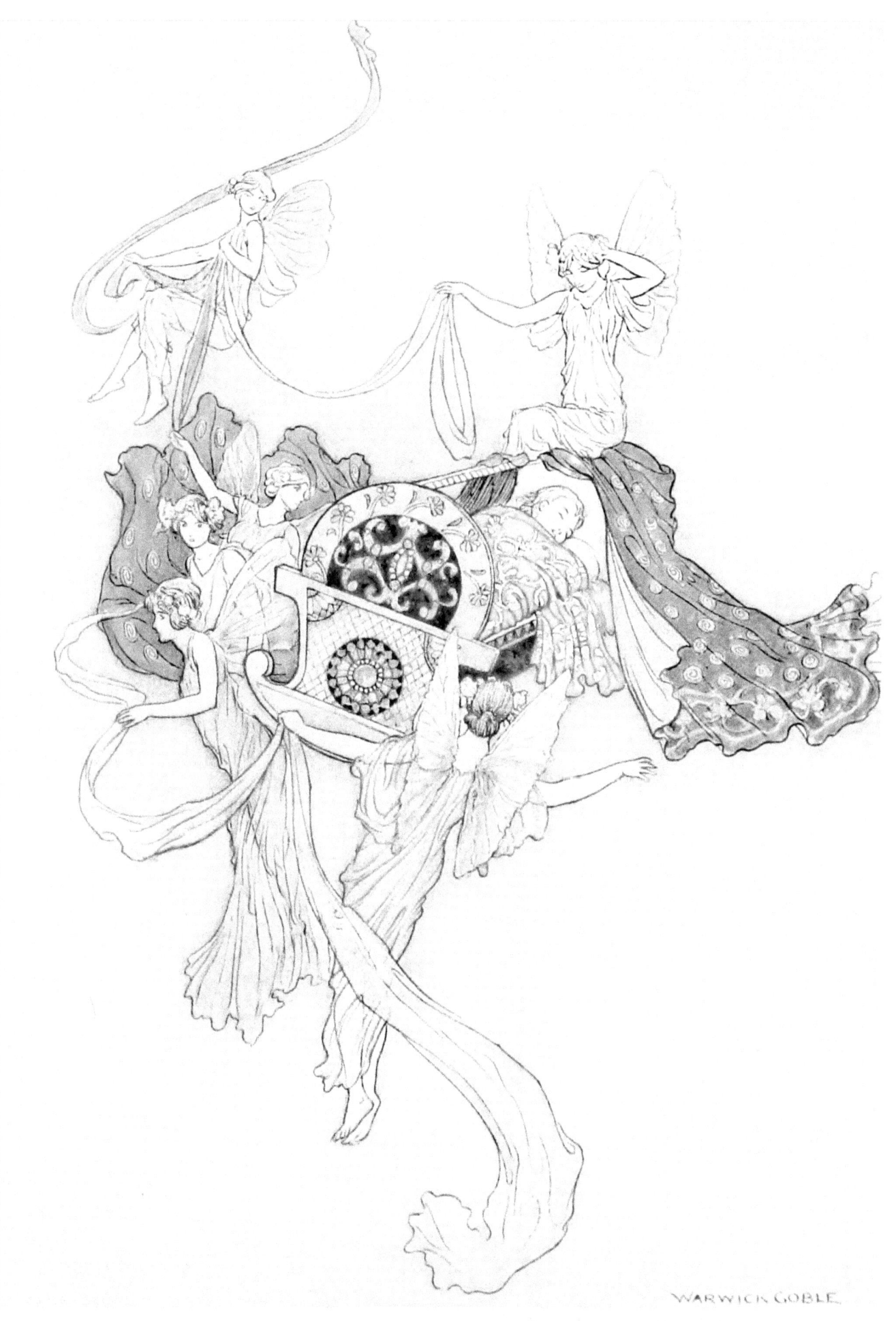

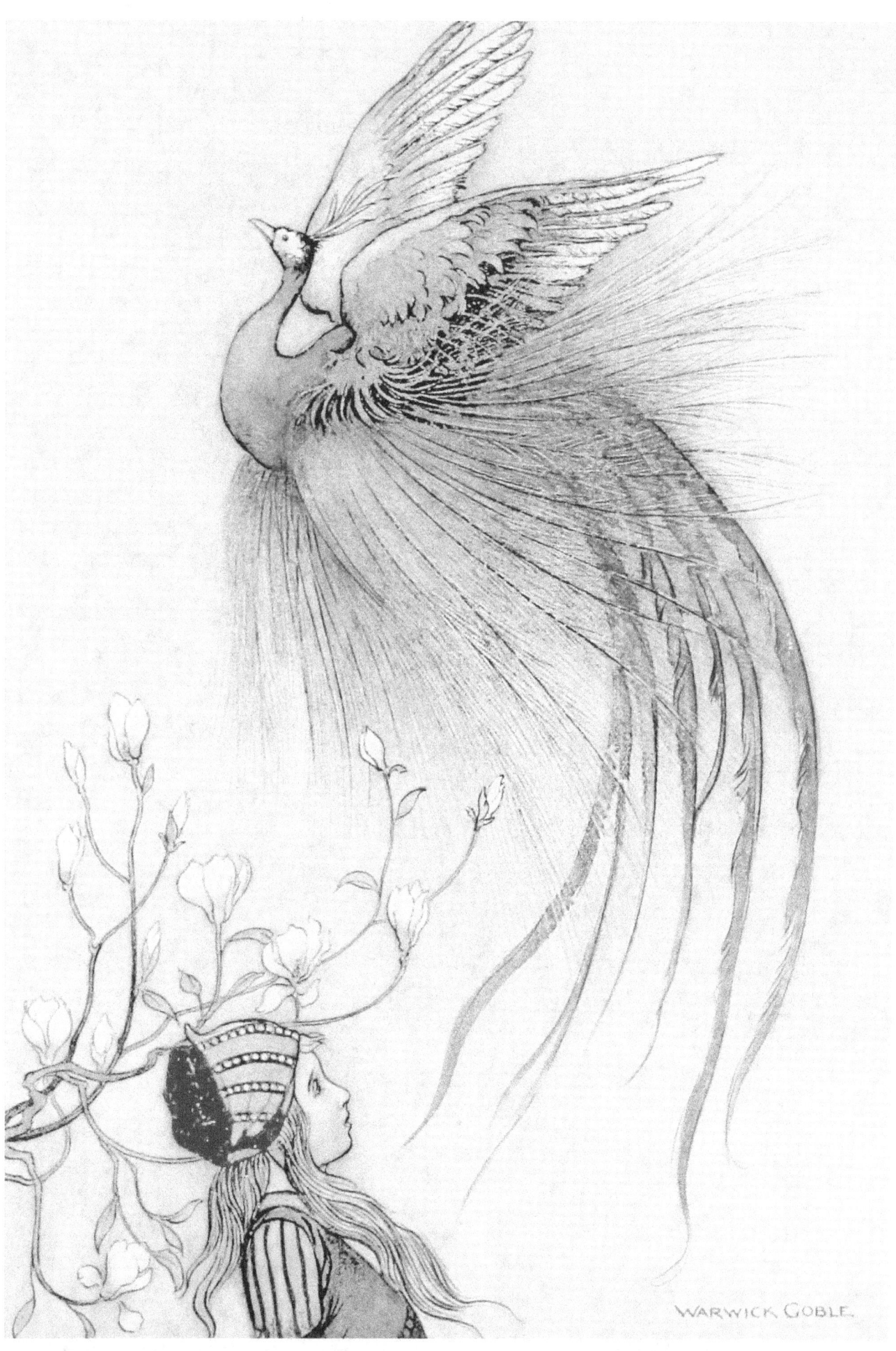

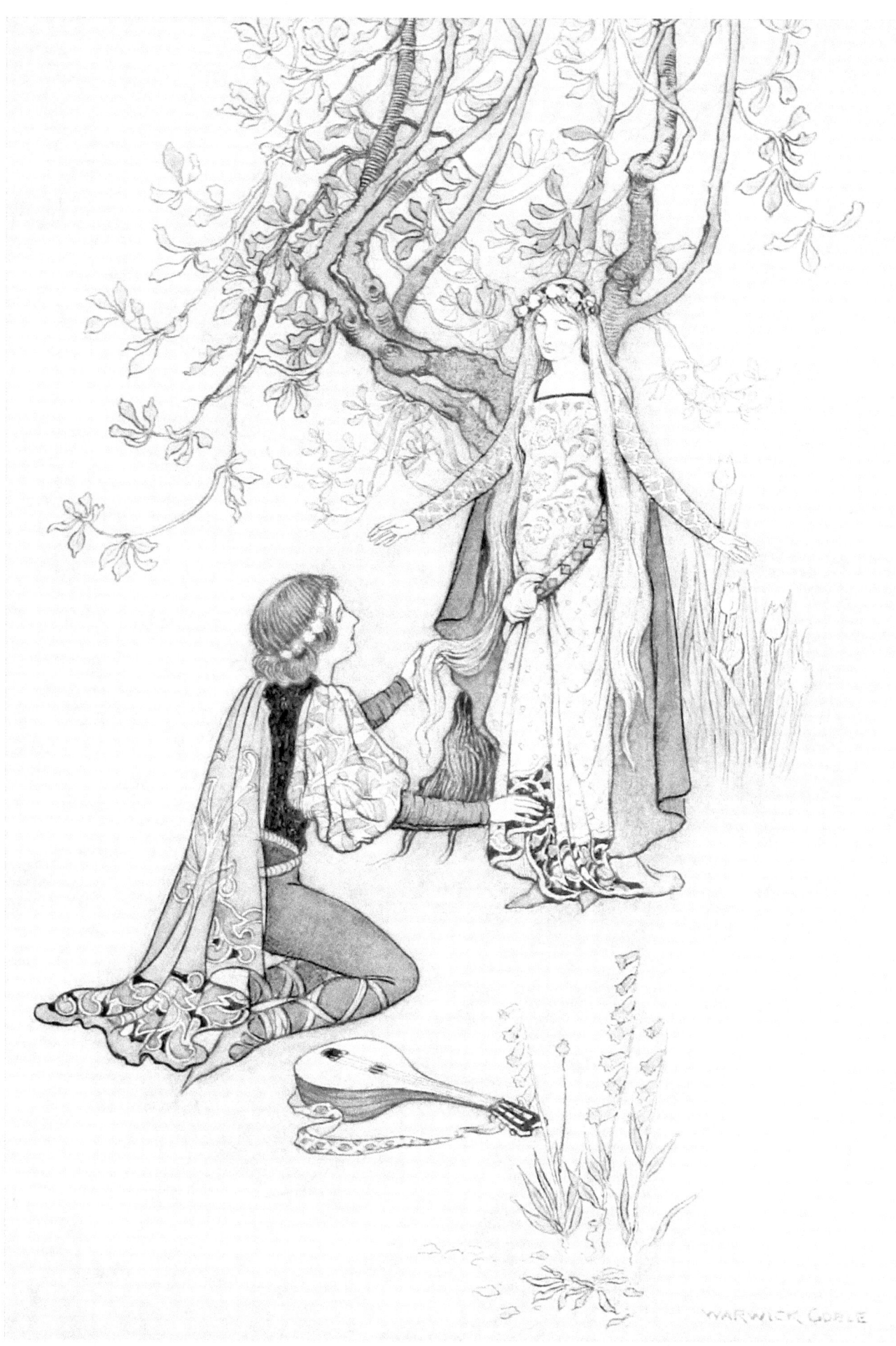

Warwick Goble's Fairy Tales

© Ligia Ortega - ColoringPress.com

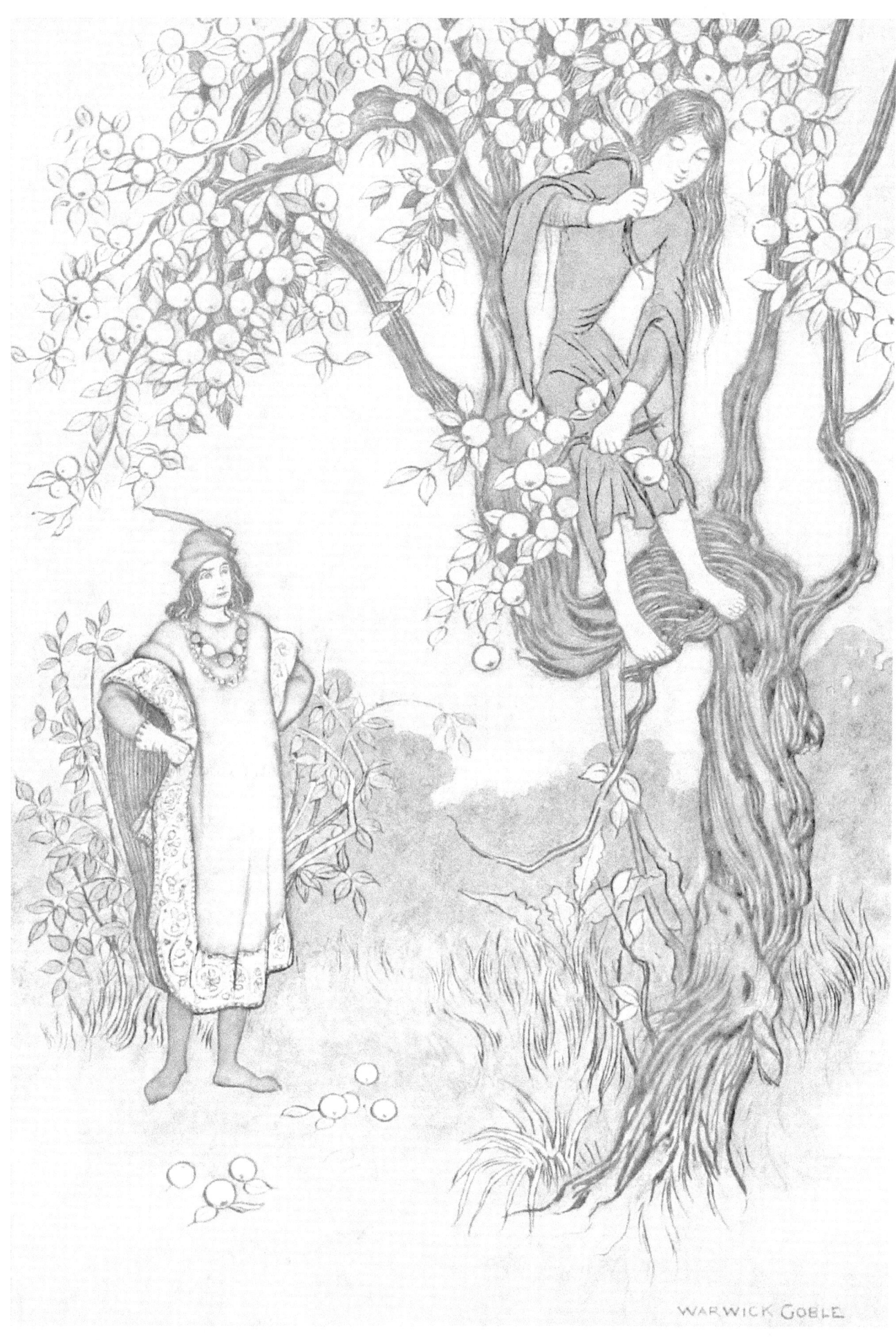

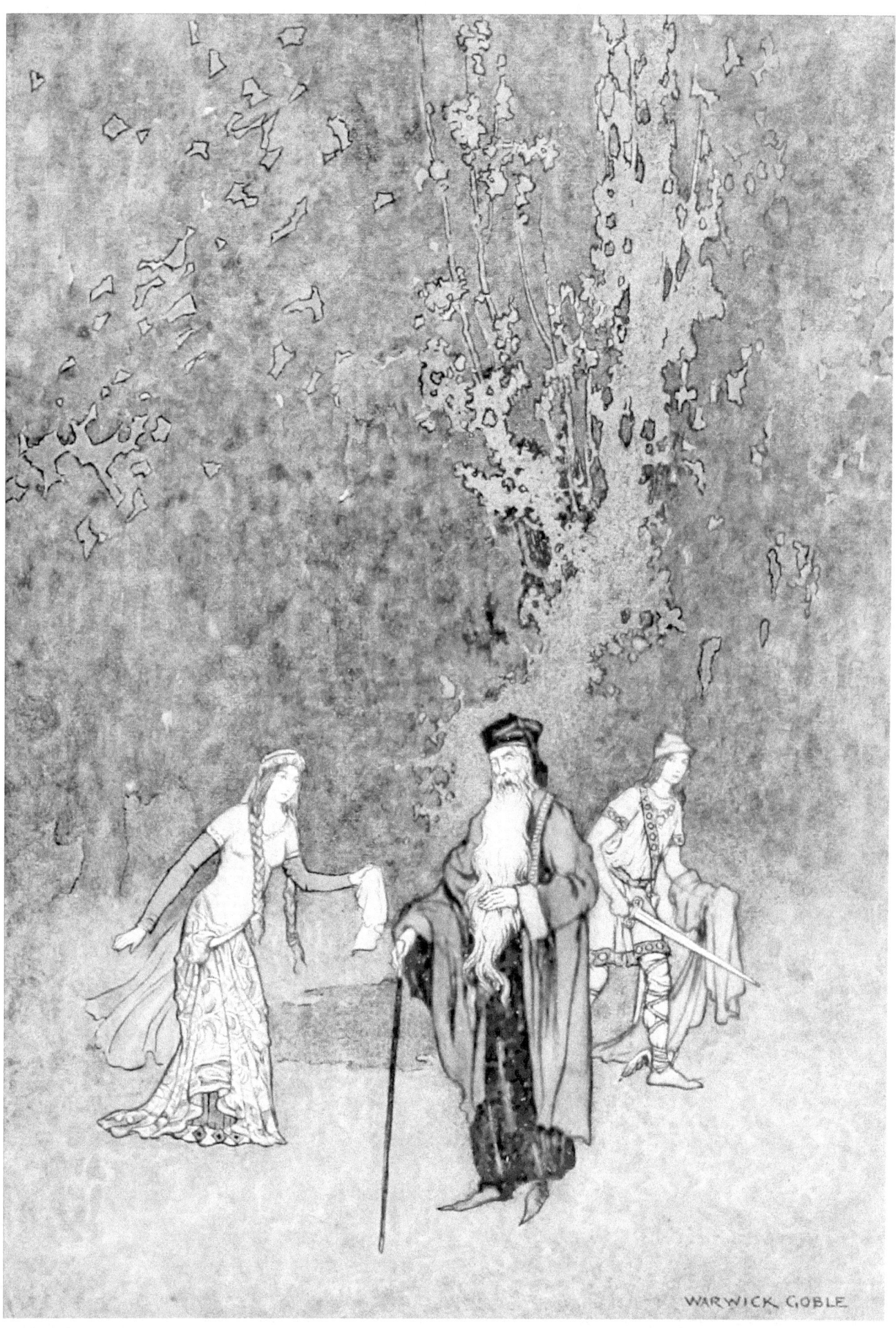

Warwick Goble's Fairy Tales

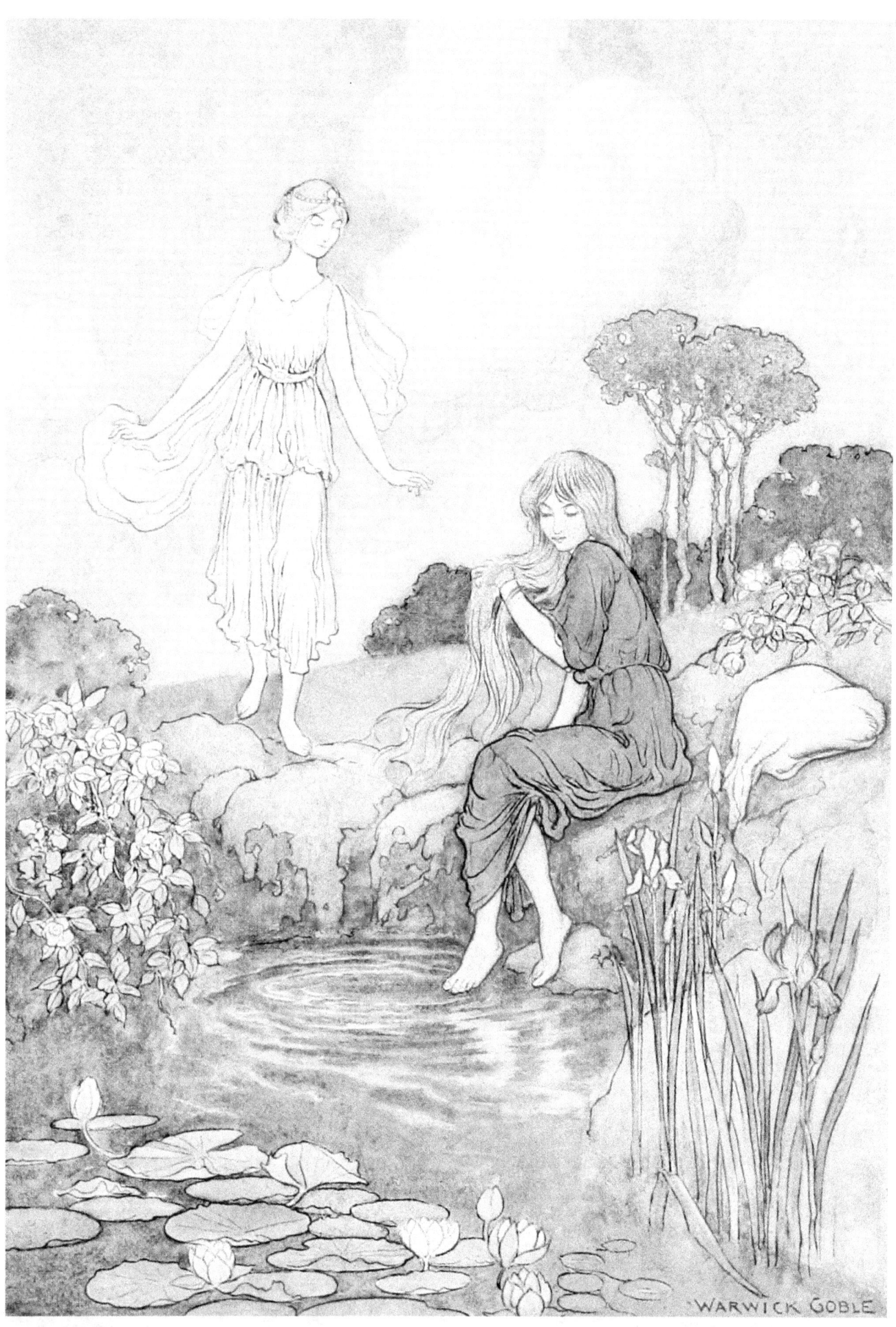

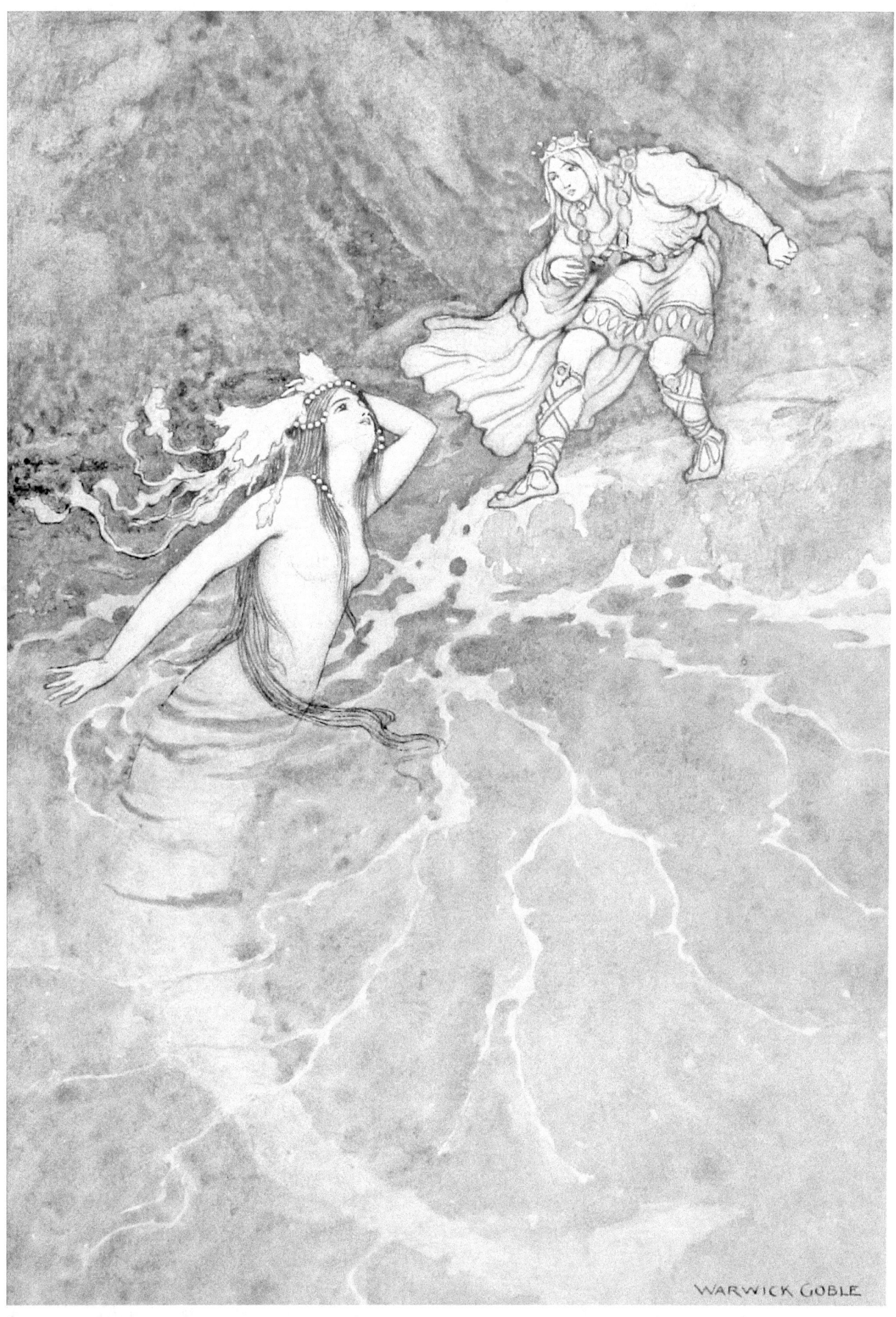

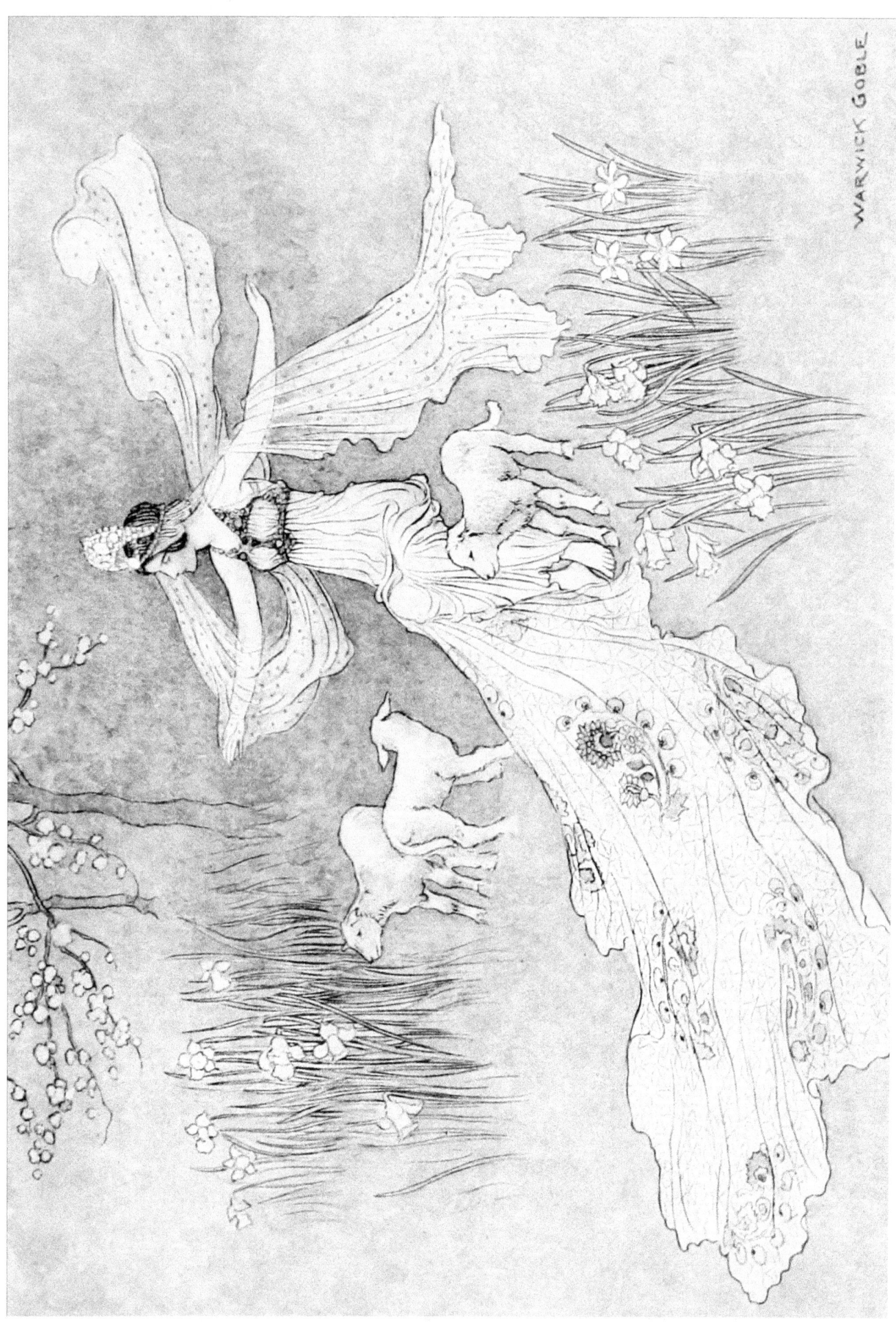

Warwick Goble's Fairy Tales © Ligia Ortega - ColoringPress.com

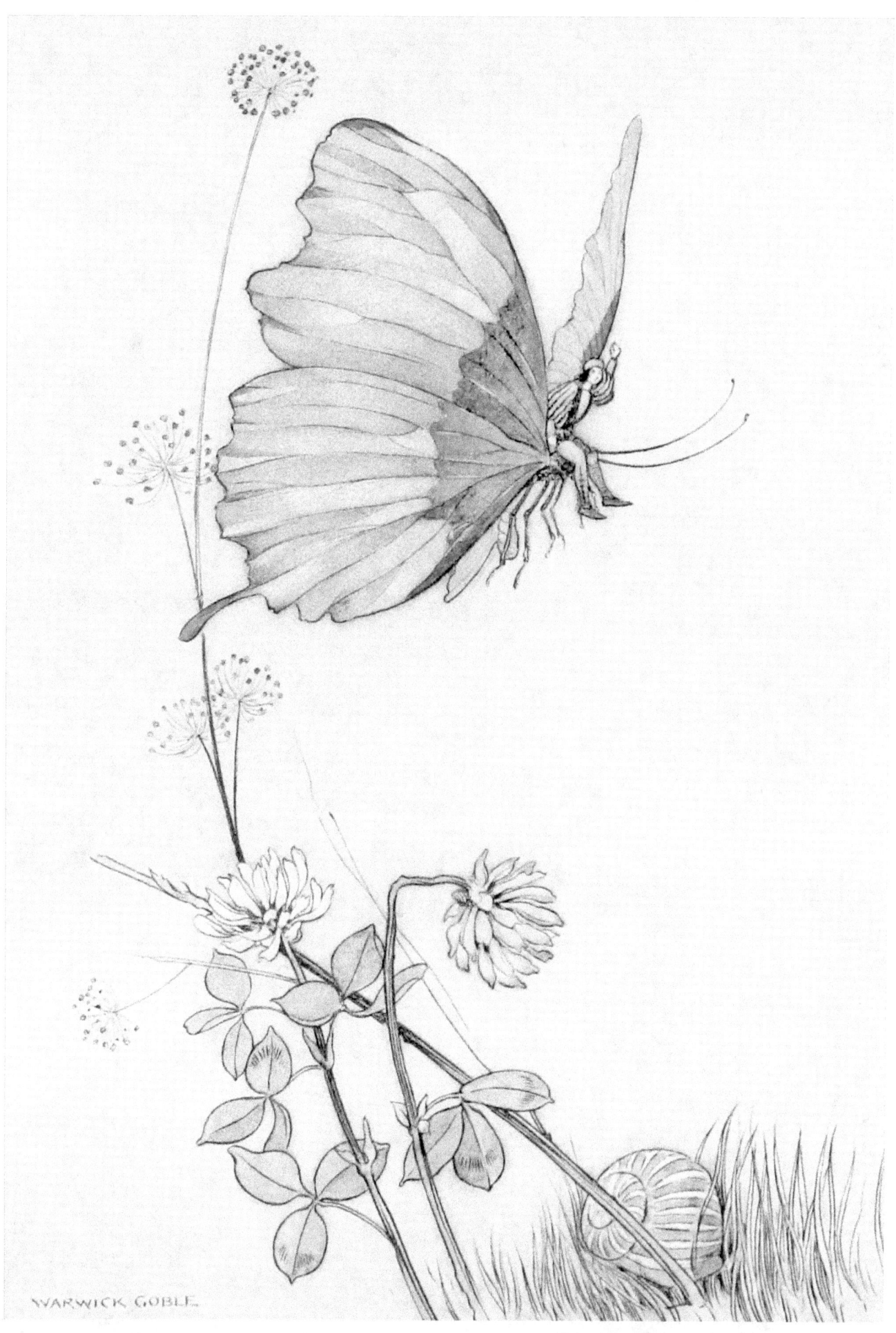

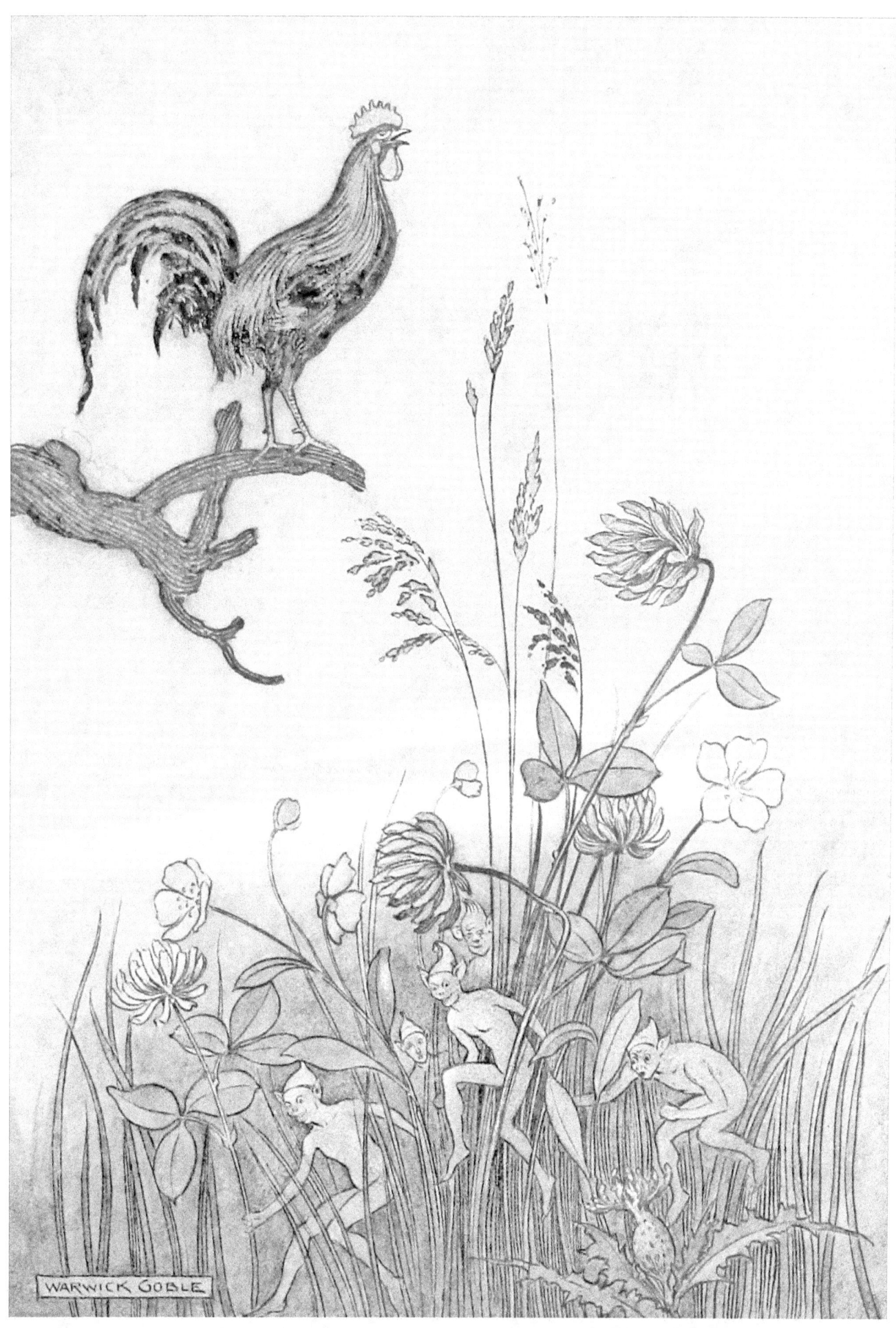

Warwick Goble's Fairy Tales

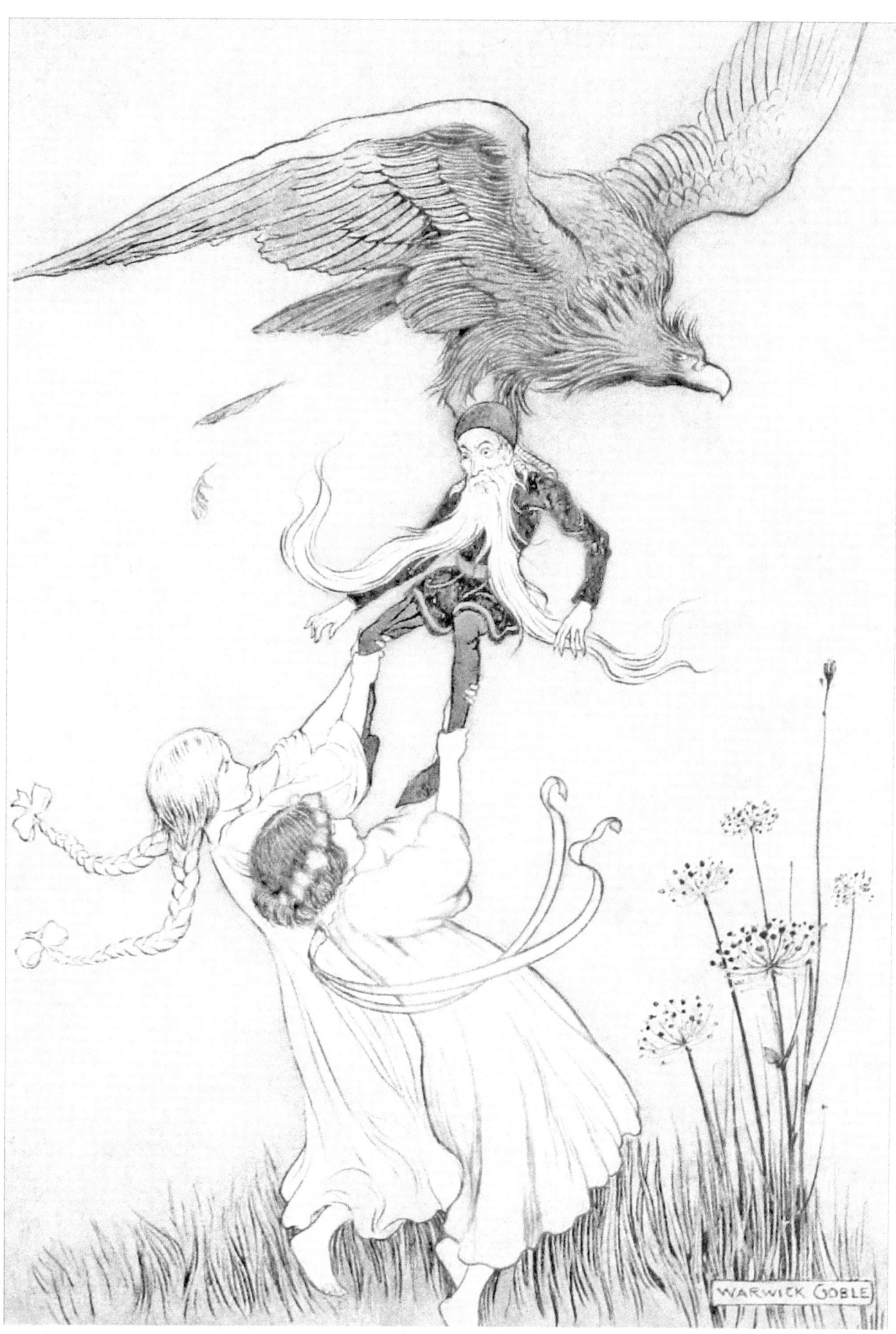

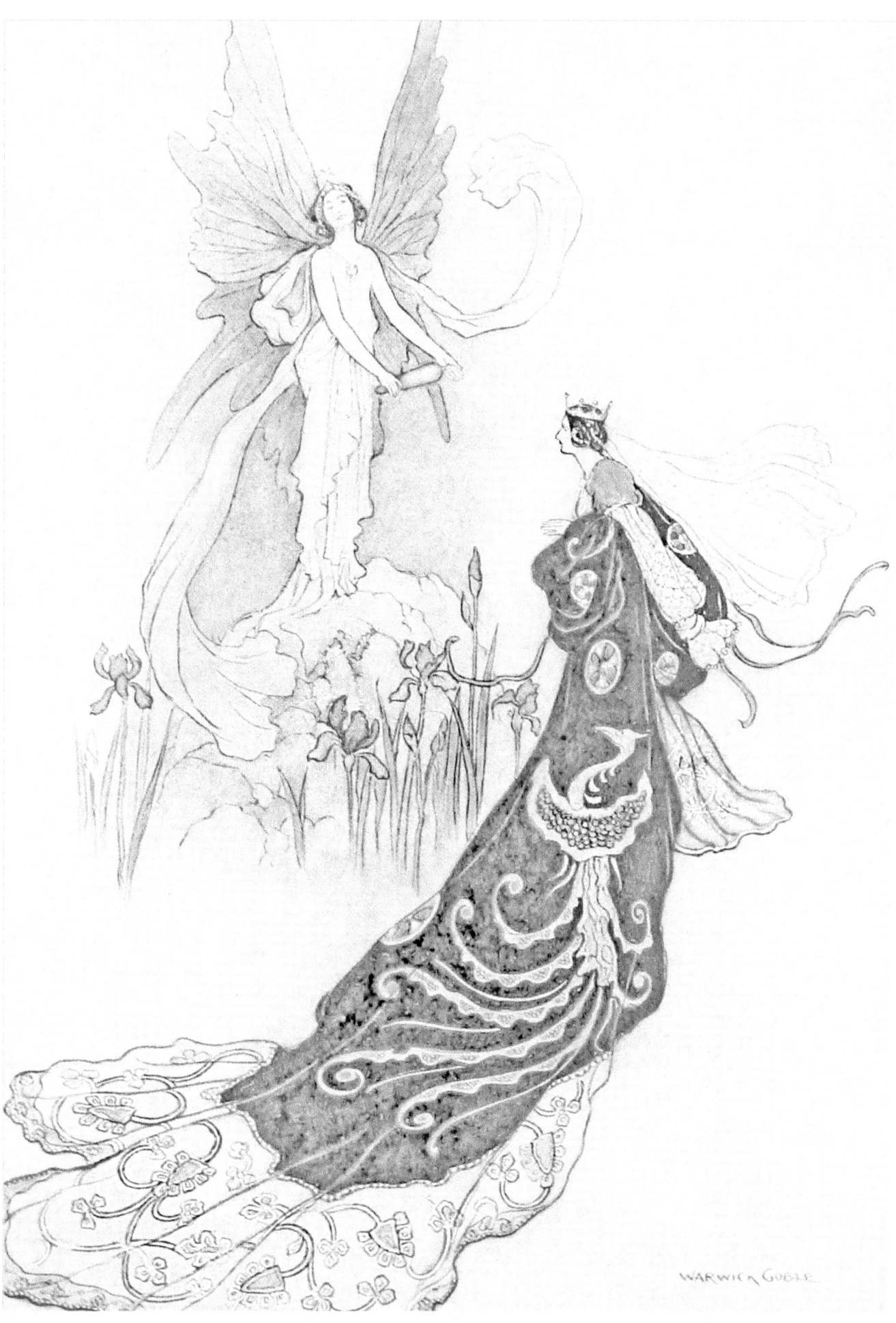

Warwick Goble's Fairy Tales

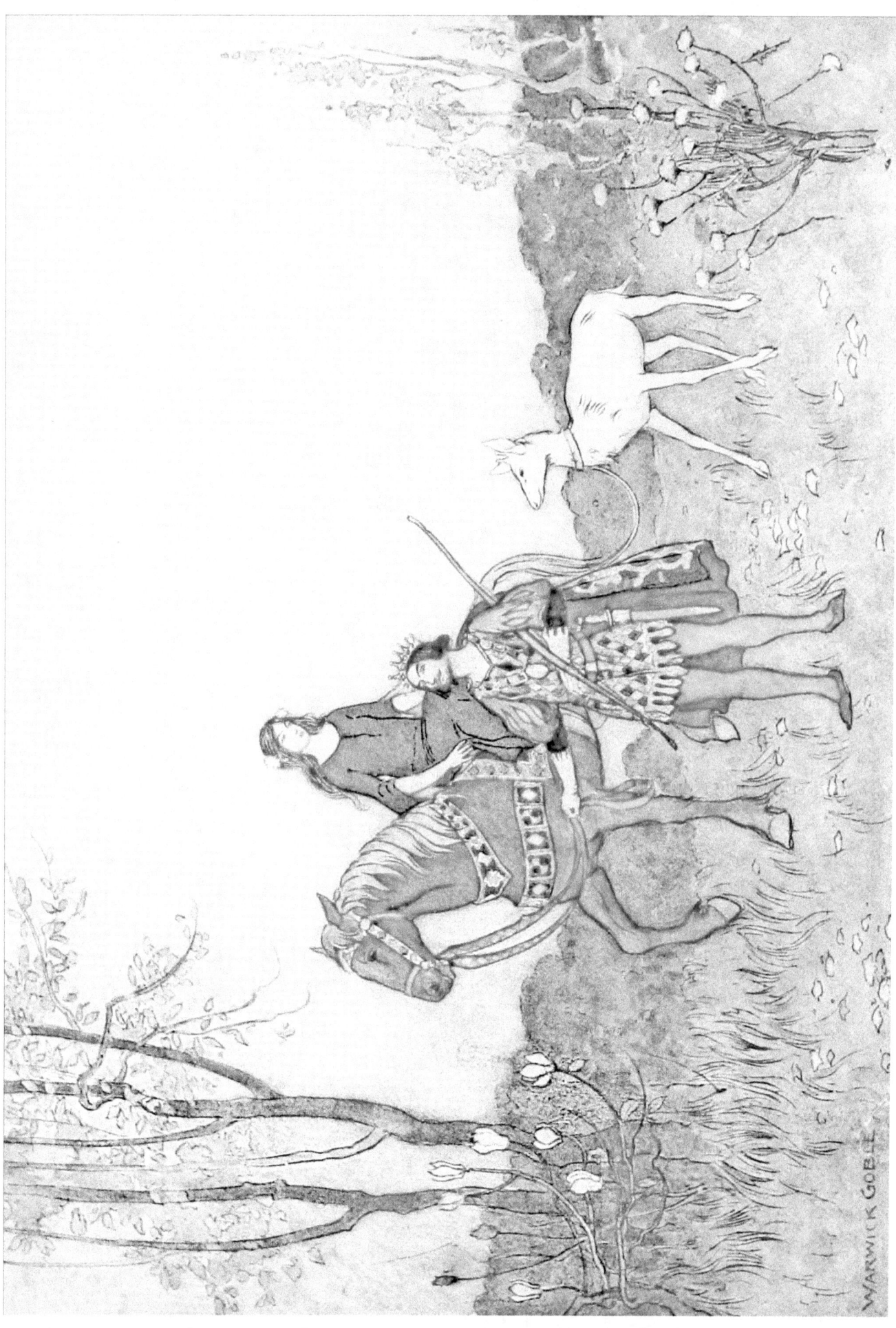

Warwick Goble's Fairy Tales

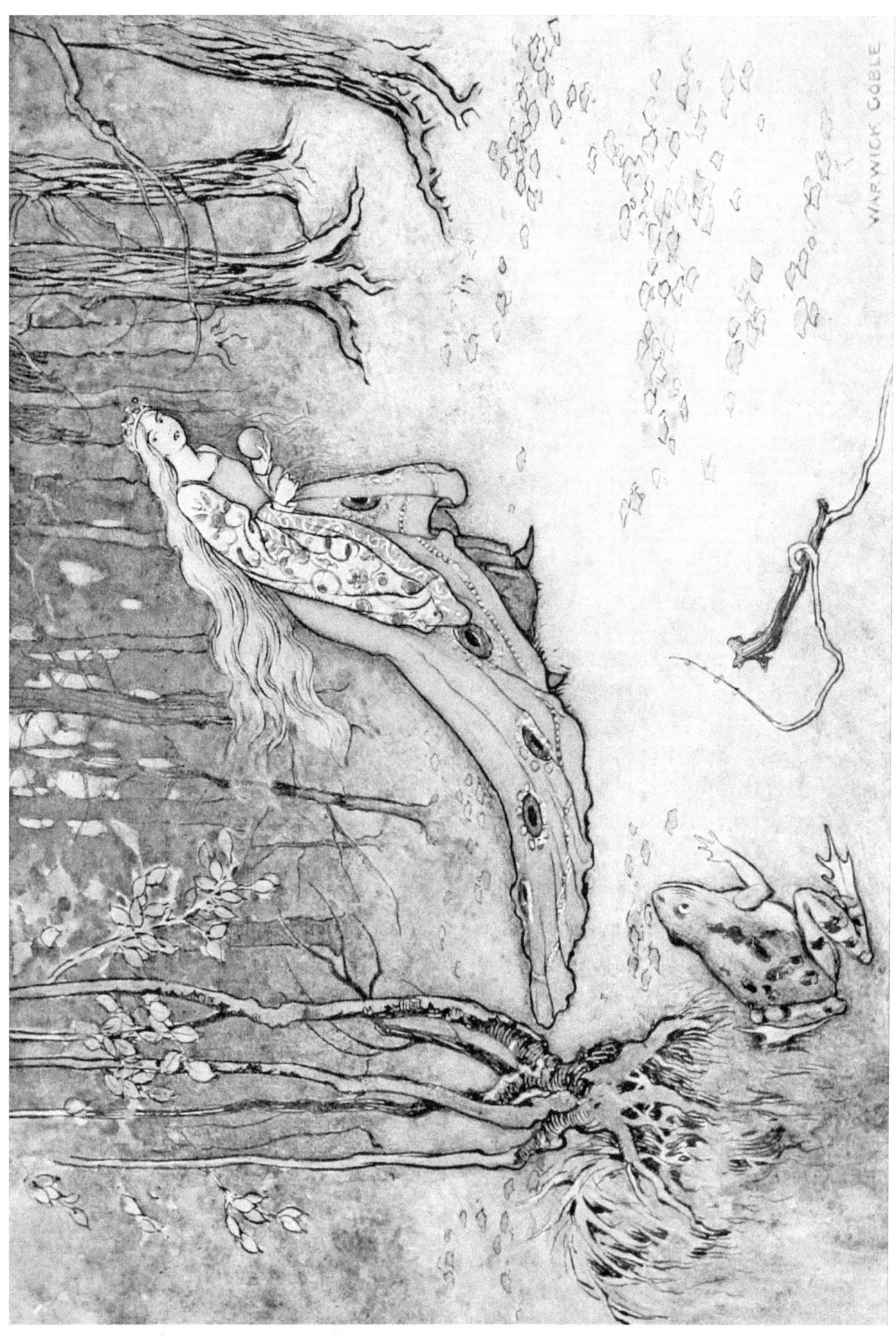

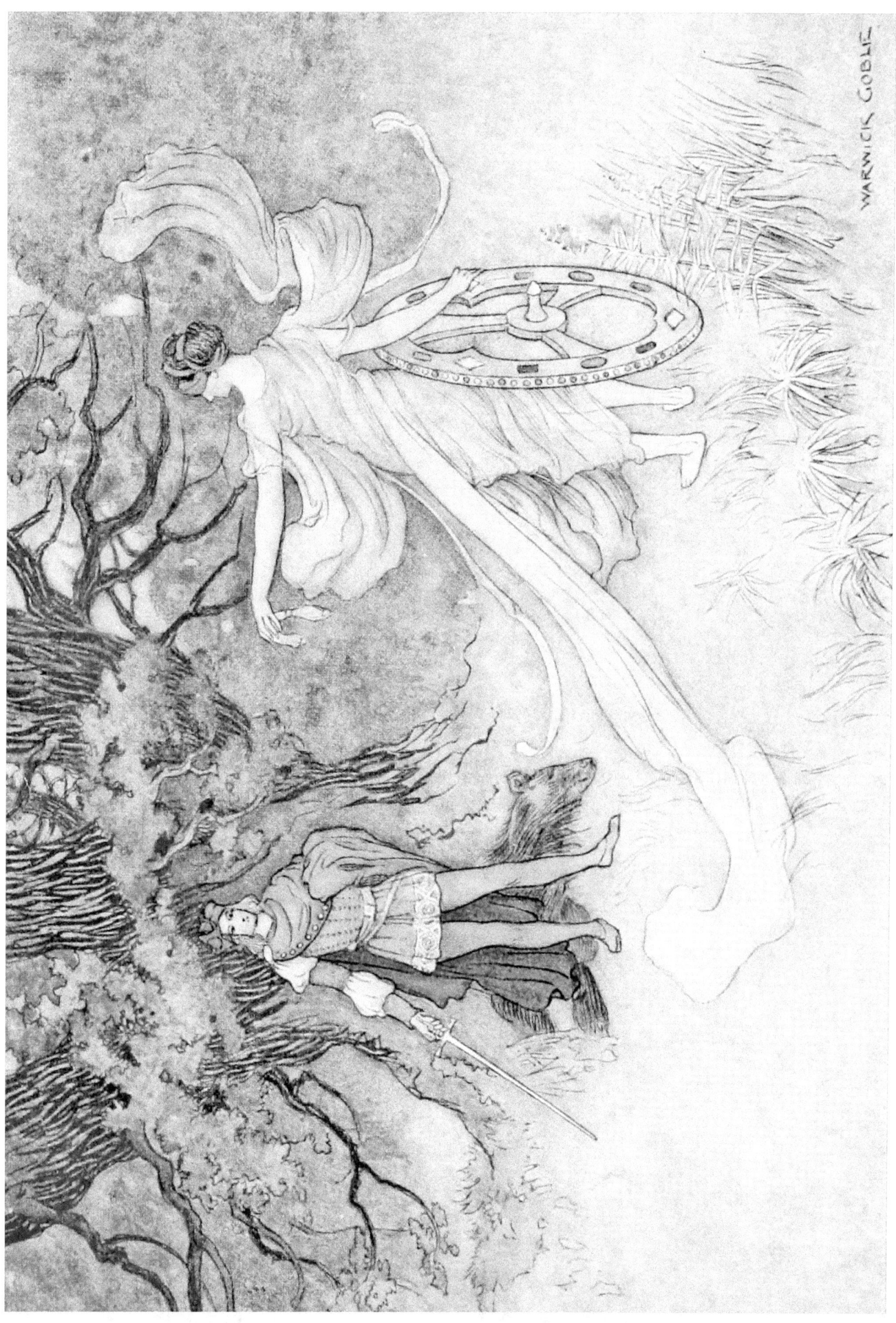

Warwick Goble's Fairy Tales

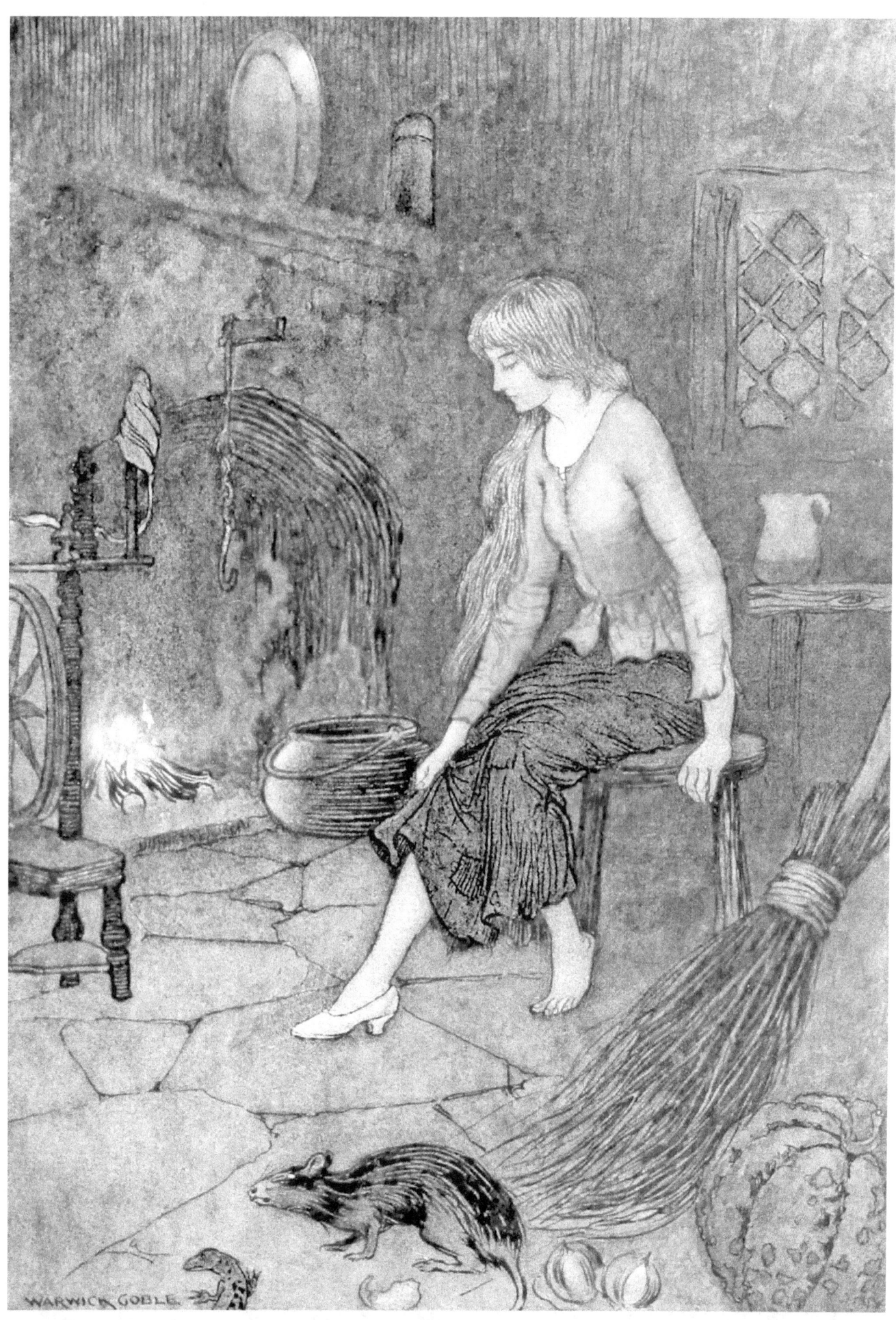

Warwick Goble's Fairy Tales

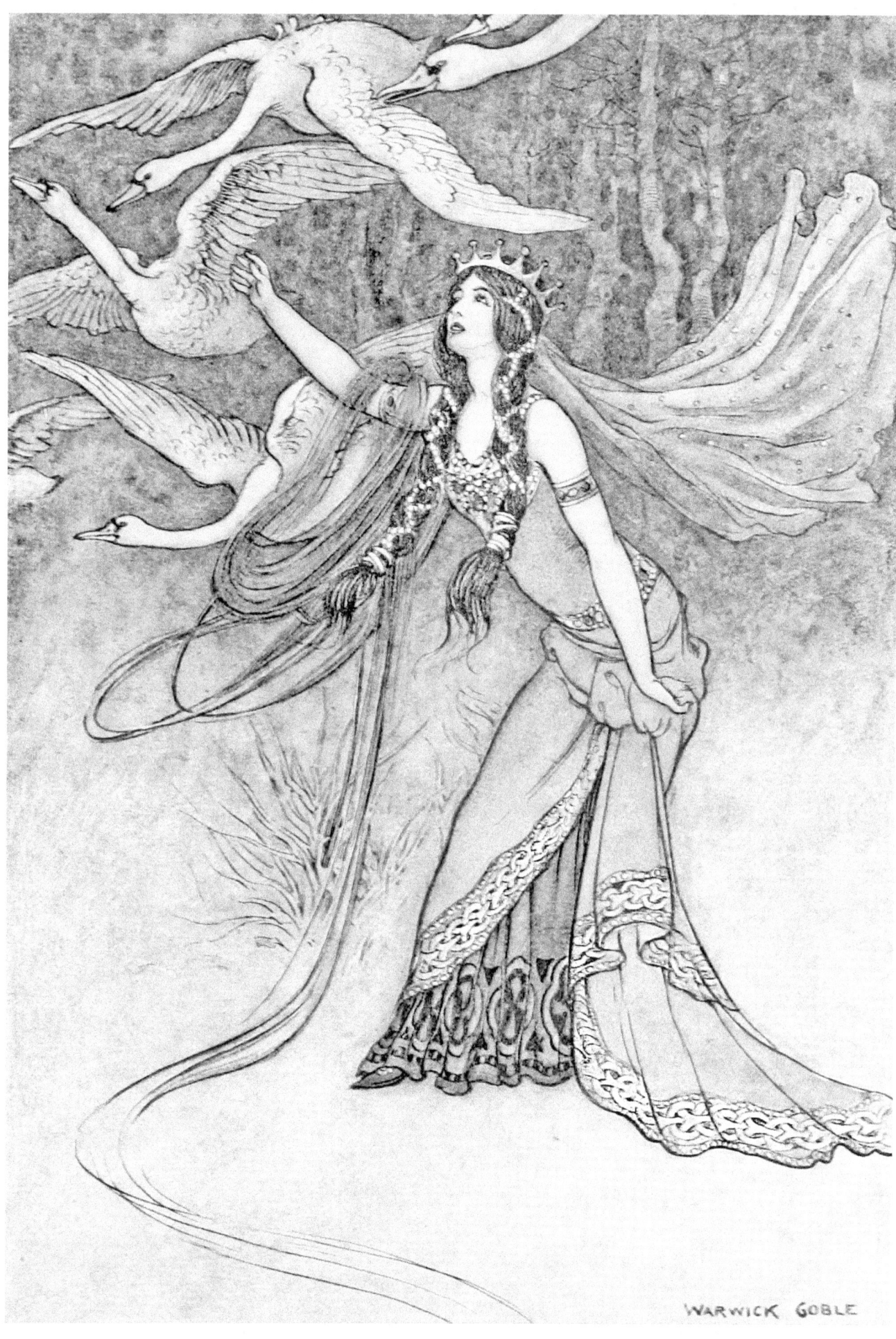

Warwick Goble's Fairy Tales

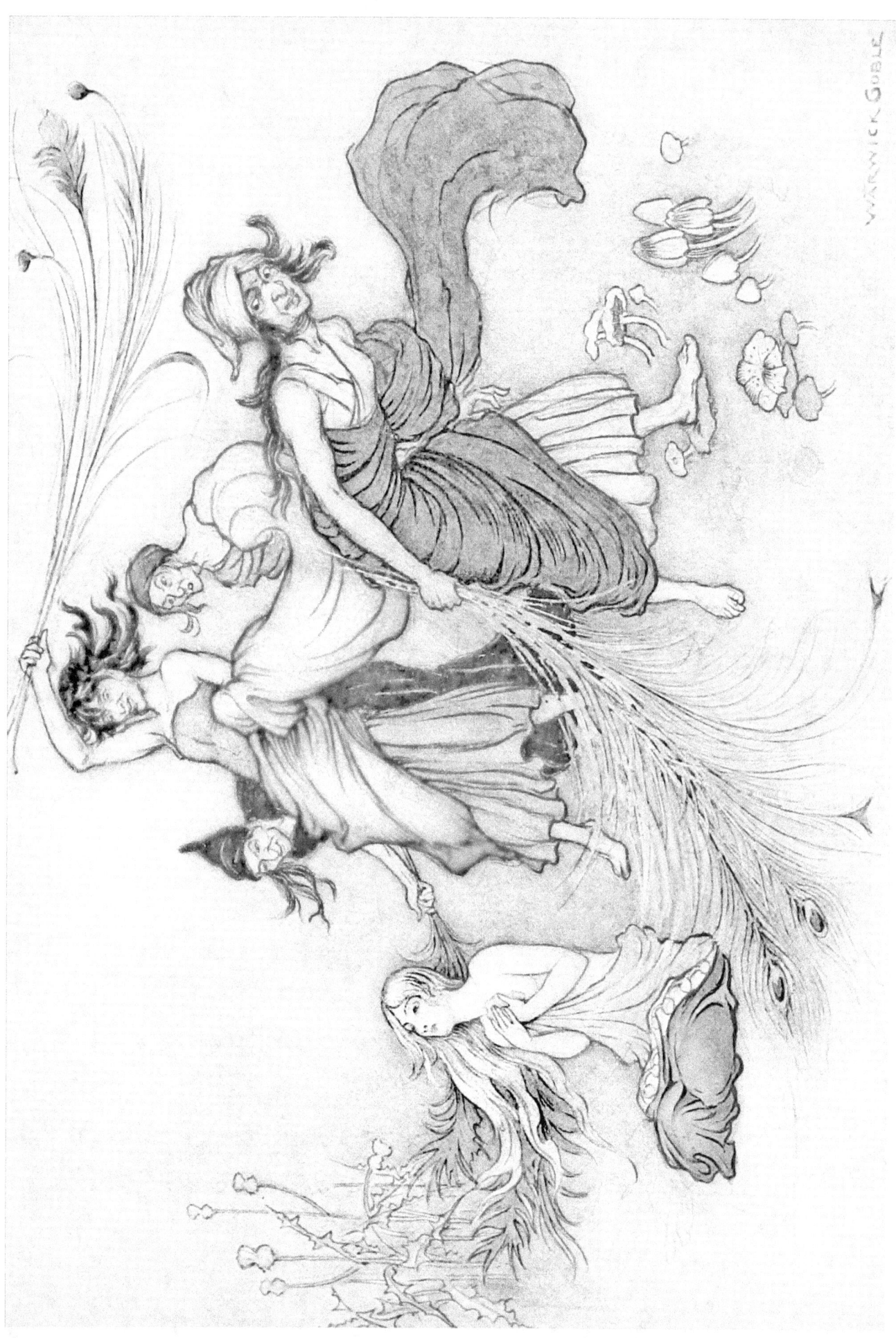

Warwick Goble's Fairy Tales © Ligia Ortega - ColoringPress.com

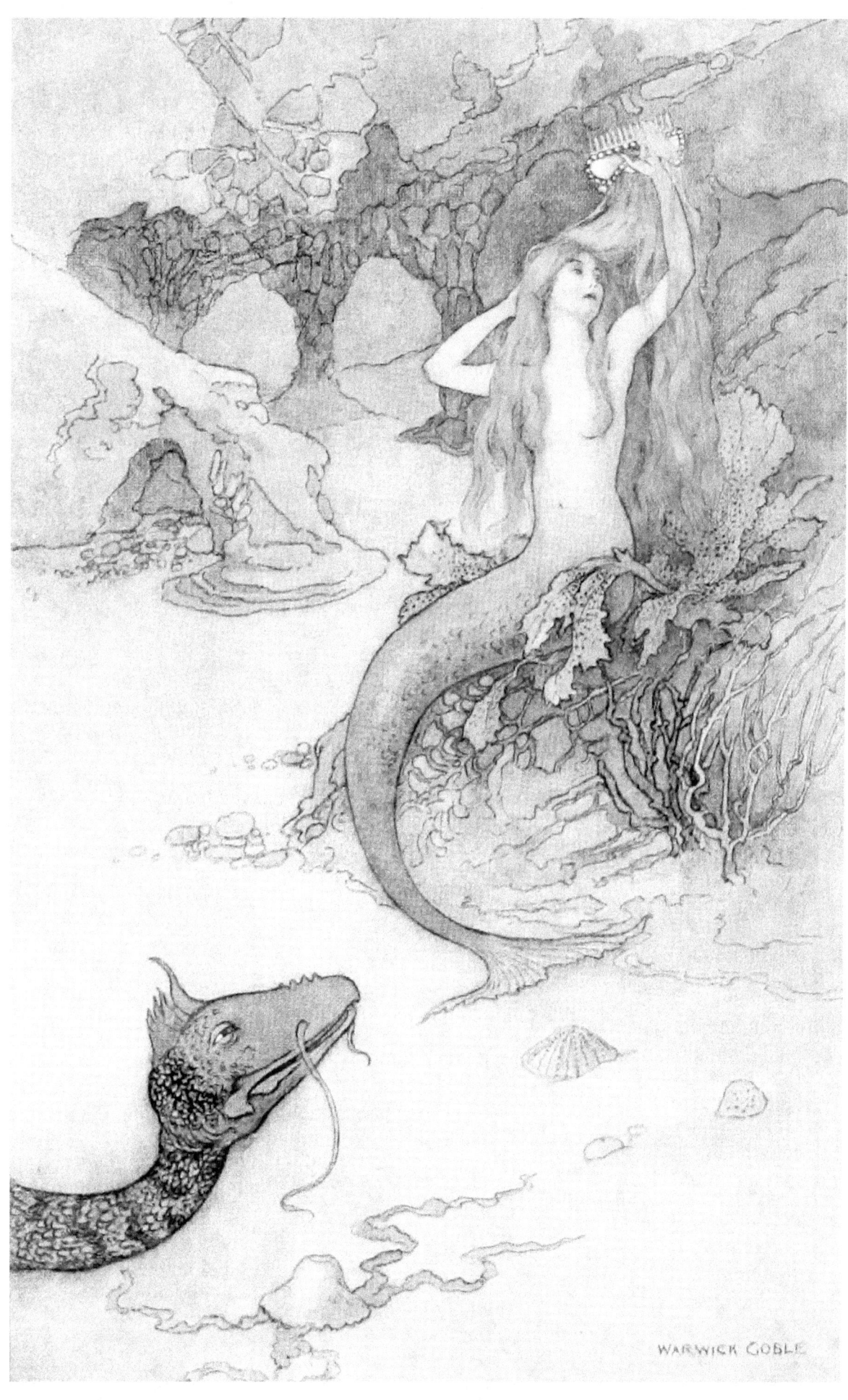

Warwick Goble's Fairy Tales

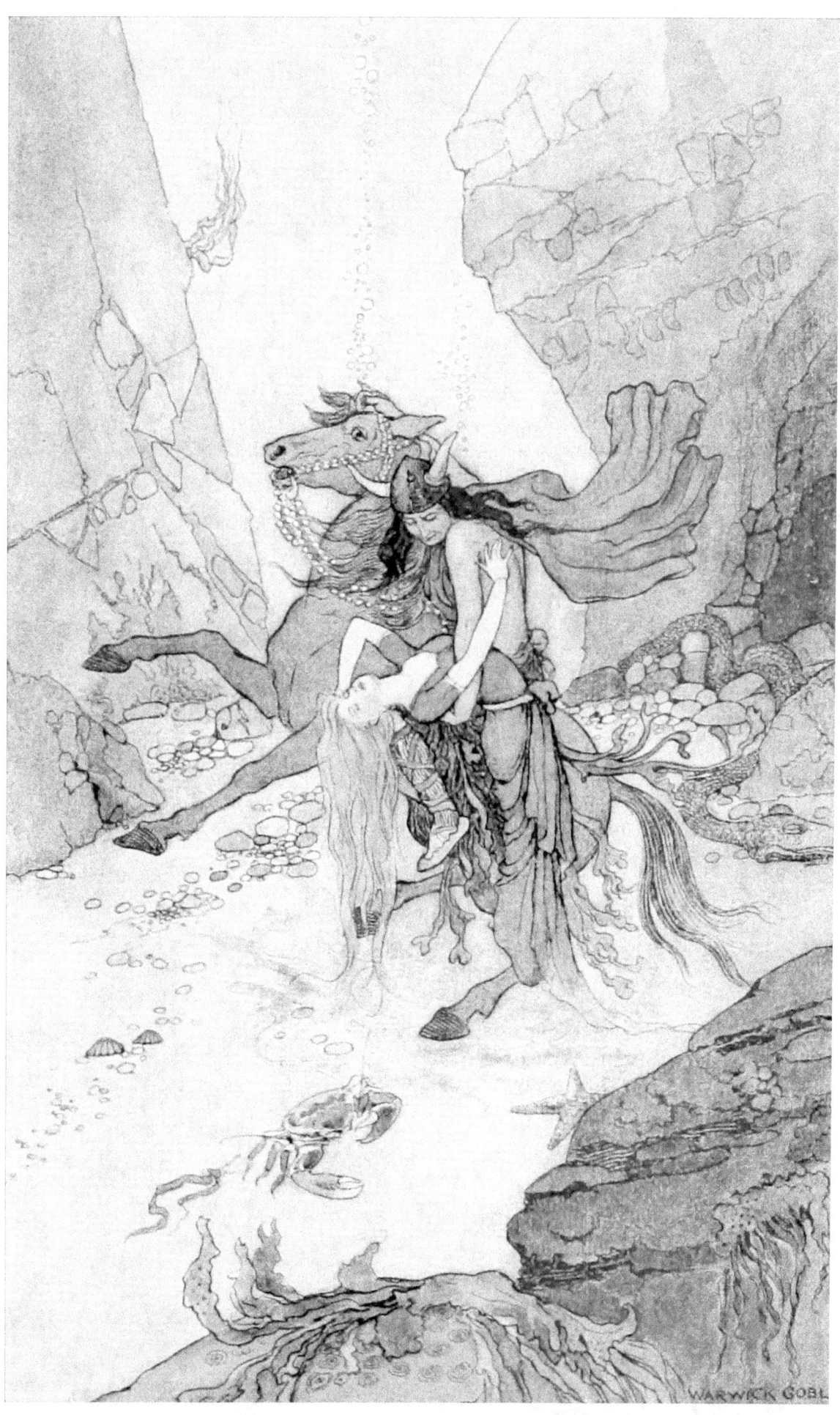

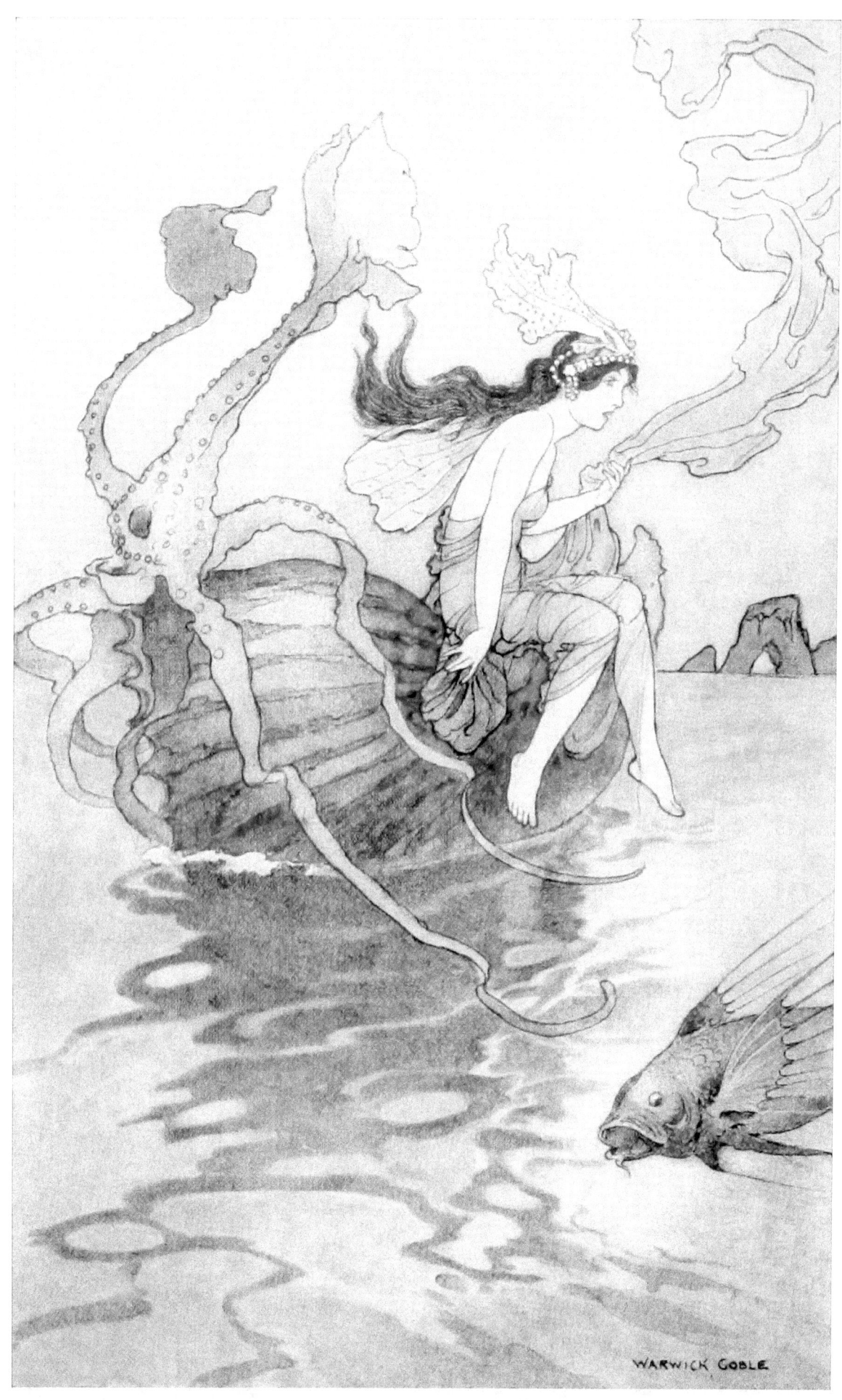

Warwick Goble's Fairy Tales

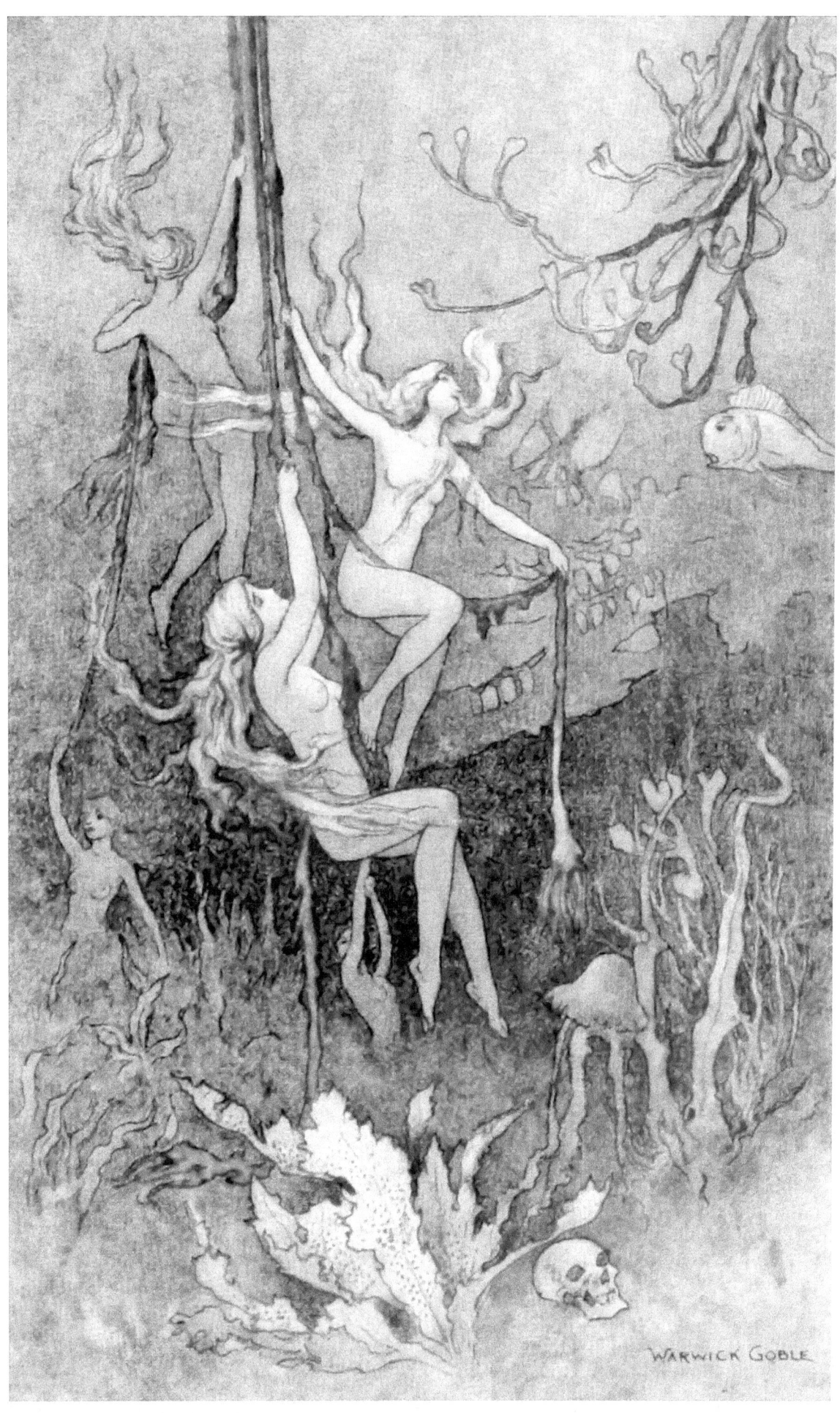

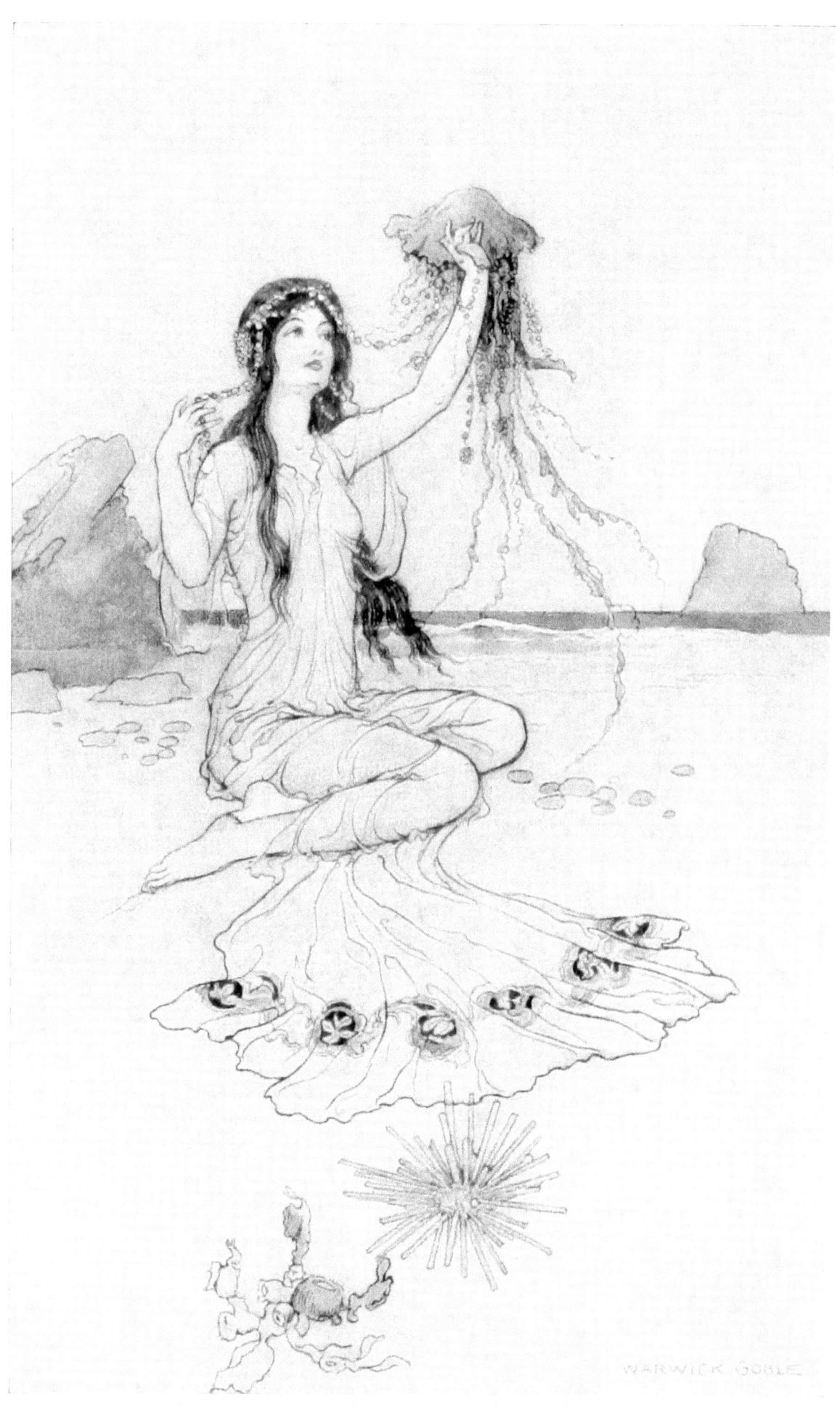

Bonus Pages

In addition to the *Vintage Grayscale Adult Coloring Book* series, I have been working on other coloring books for adults. The following coloring pages are from books I have published under Coloring Press.

The first images are samples from Volumes 1-3 of my *Coloring Gifts*™ Book Series, *Coloring Gifts*™: *Gifts of Thanks*; *Coloring Gifts*™: *Gifts of Encouragement*; and *Coloring Gifts*™: *Gifts of Friendship*. These themed adult coloring books each have 24 original hand drawn pages printed in two different sizes (full size and craft size, approx. 5x7") plus nine coordinating bookmarks. Pages can be colored and given as is, or framed, turned into cards, or made into bookmarks using the included instructions. These pages can also be used to aid prayer or meditation with the enclosed instructions to reap the full health benefits of coloring and gratitude, encouragement, and friendship. I am already working on the next volume of *Coloring Gifts*™. Visit ColoringPress.com for more information on *Coloring Gifts*™.

The fourth and fifth images are from my *Vintage Grayscale Adult Coloring Book* Series, Volume 1 *Arthur Rackham's Fairies and Nymphs* and Volume 3, *Bevalet's Hummingbirds and Flowers*. I am already working on Volume 4 of this series. Visit ColoringPress.com for more information on grayscale coloring.

The remaining images are from my *Simple Kaleidoscopes* coloring books. I took on the challenge of making kaleidoscope images by hand rather than having software generated ones. It was fun watching them come to life from my own hand-drawn black and white coloring image. These kaleidoscopes are published as full size 8.5x11" books and also as travel size 6x8" book. Black background versions are in the works too. I published these books in response to colorists asking for a less intricate kaleidoscope where they could show off their shading or just have larger spaces to color. Their bold lines and larger spaces also work well for people with low vision or issues with hand control. The travel size books are perfect for taking with you to the mechanic, the dentist, the doctor's office, or any place where you may have to wait. They make the time fly by quickly and the wait a lot more pleasant, and their small size means you can usually finish coloring a page in one sitting. This series is being well received by colorists and I will be publishing additional Simple books in different themes including flowers, mandalas, and others.

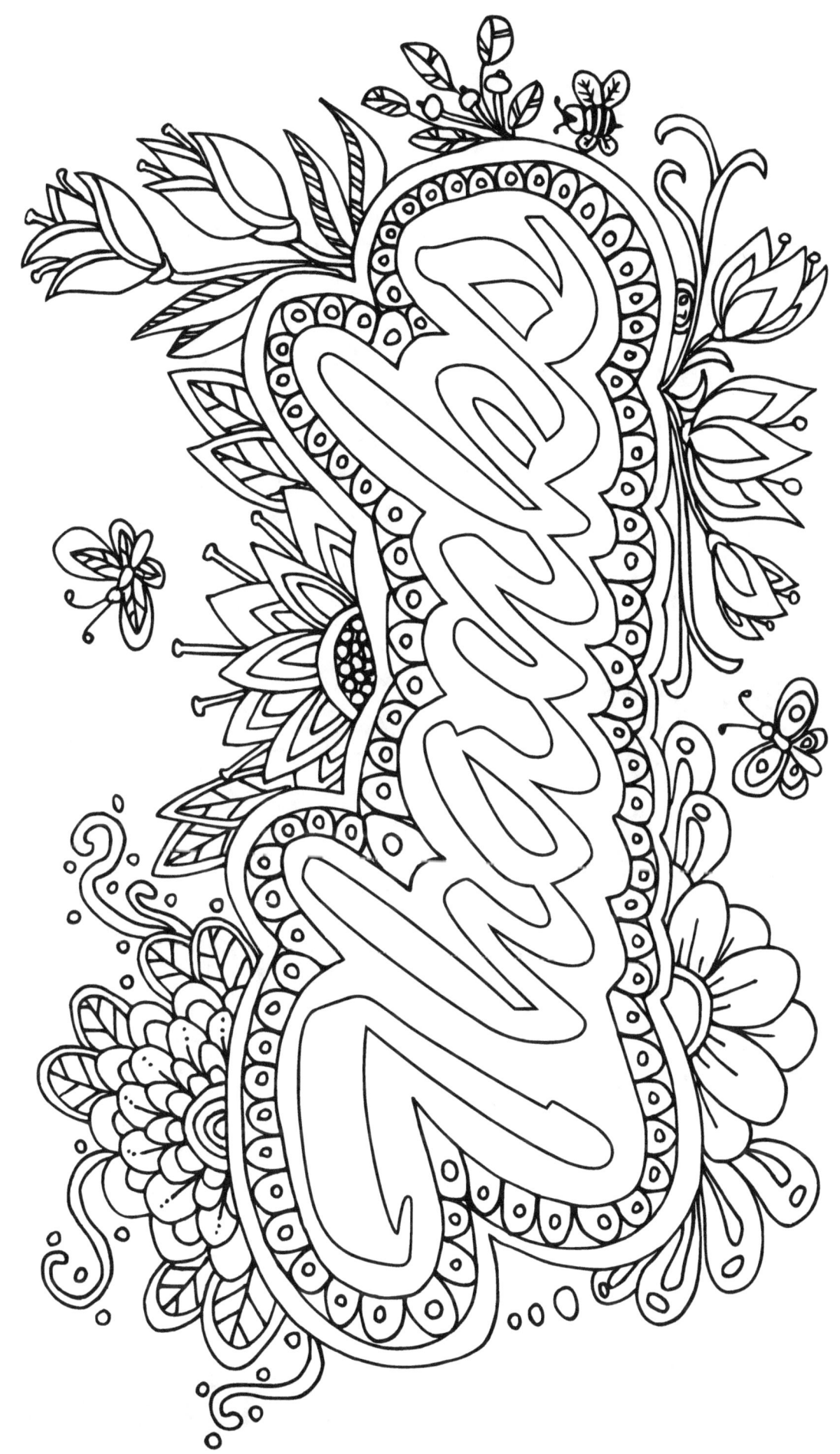

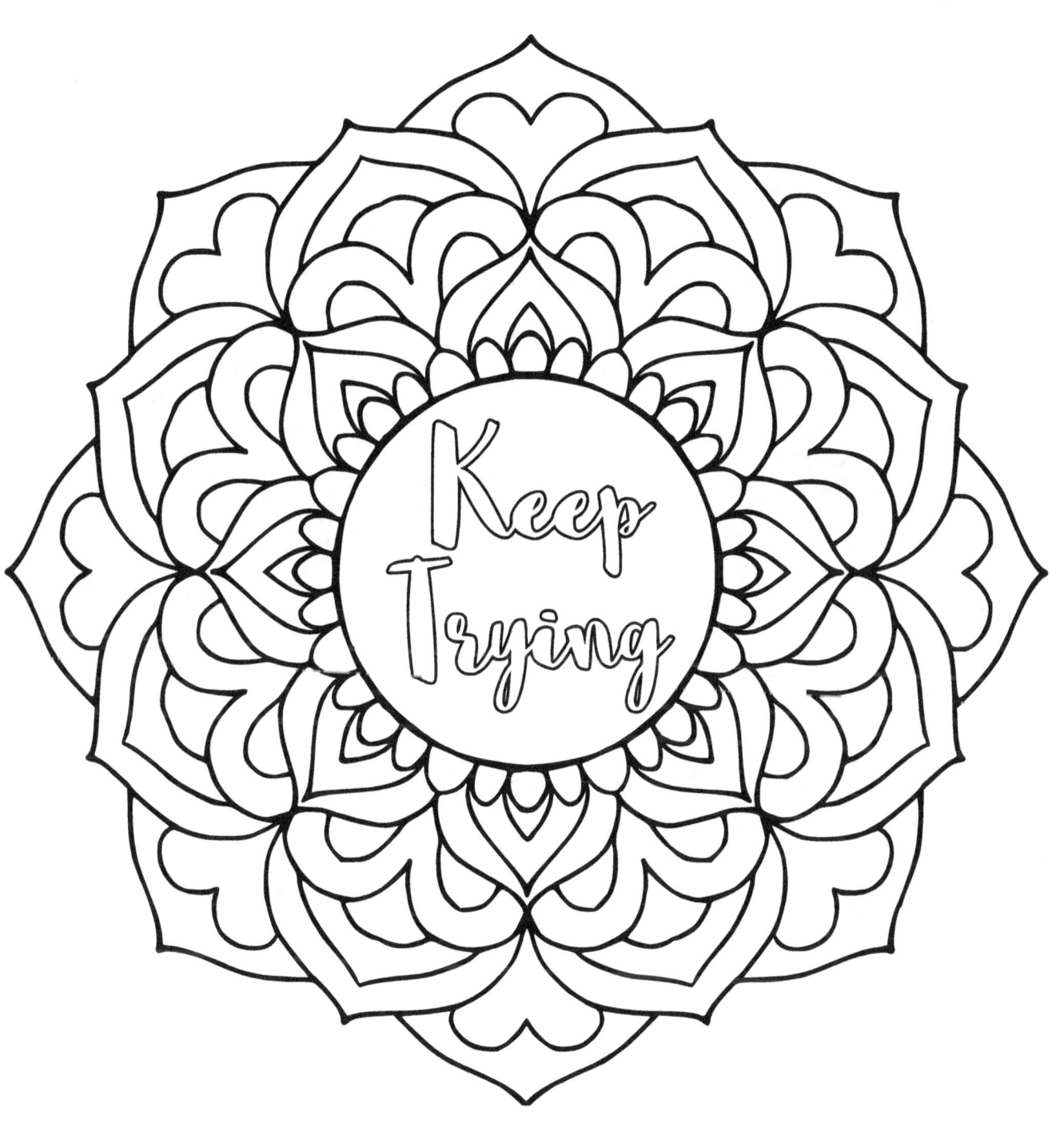

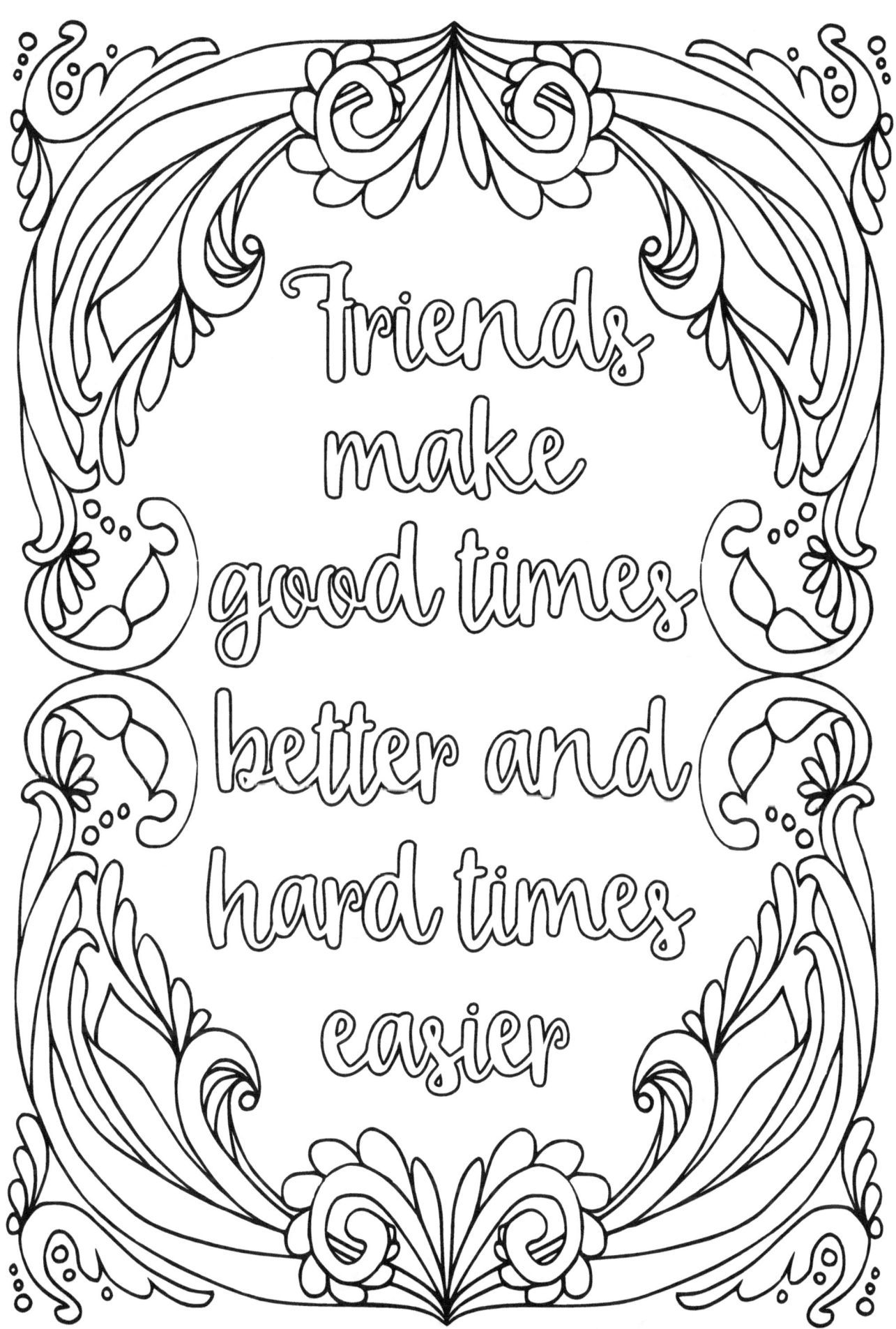

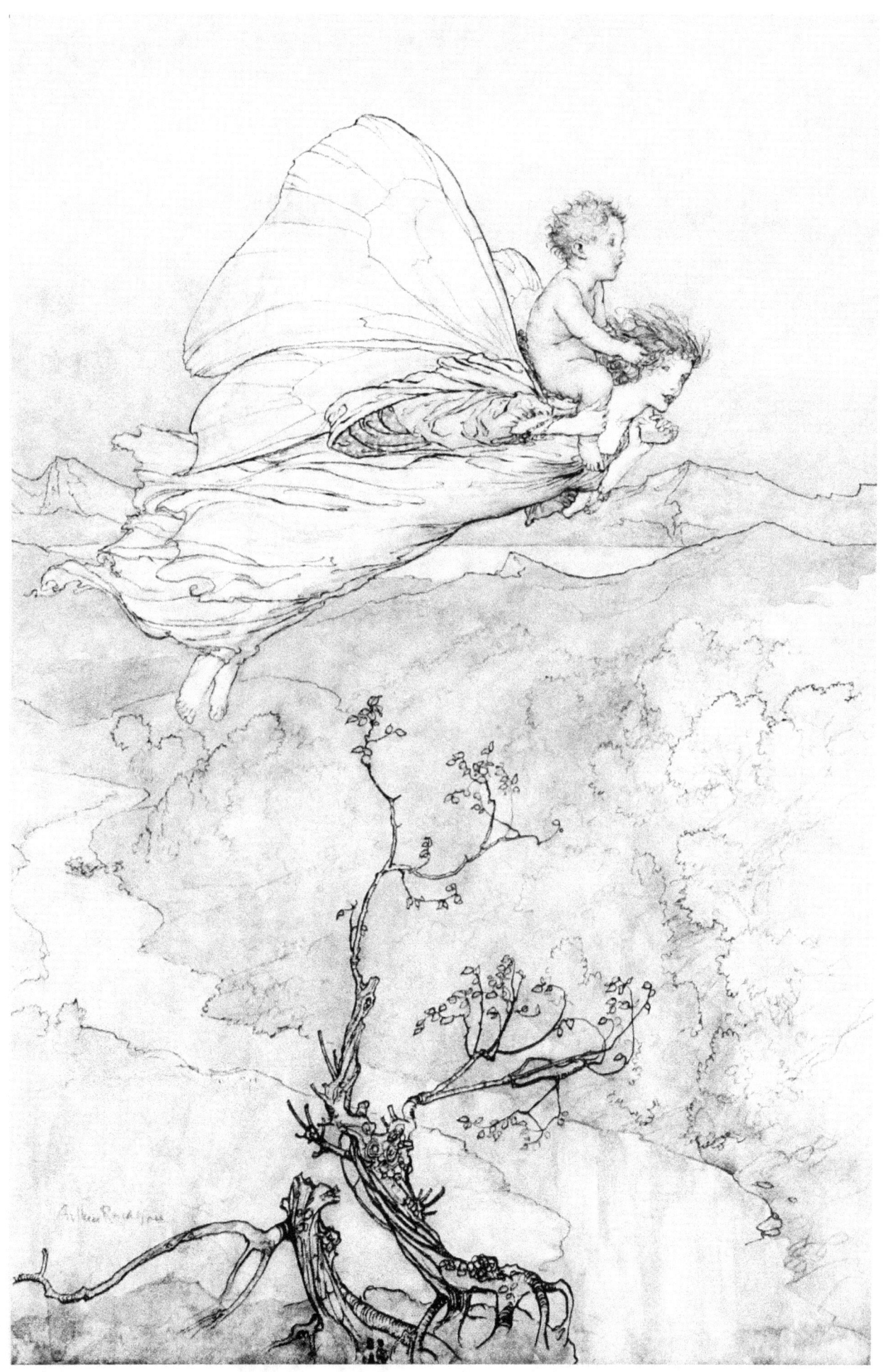

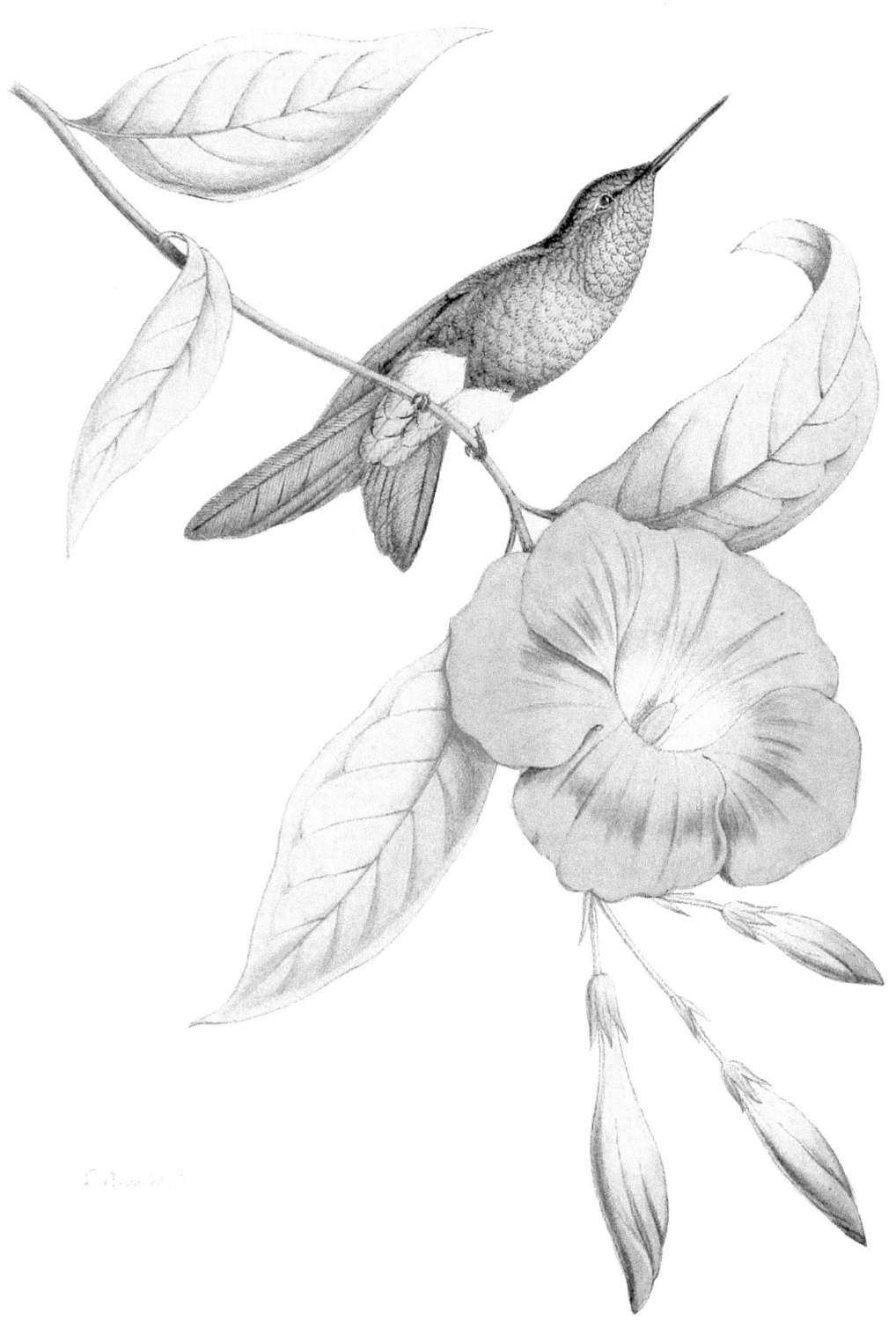

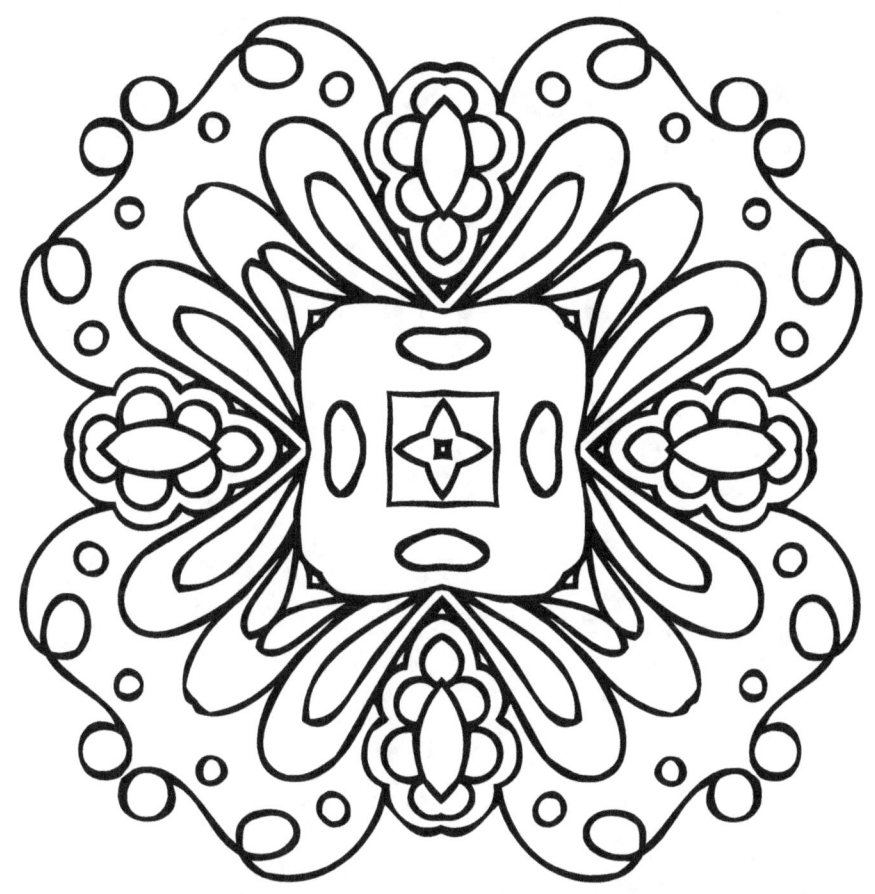

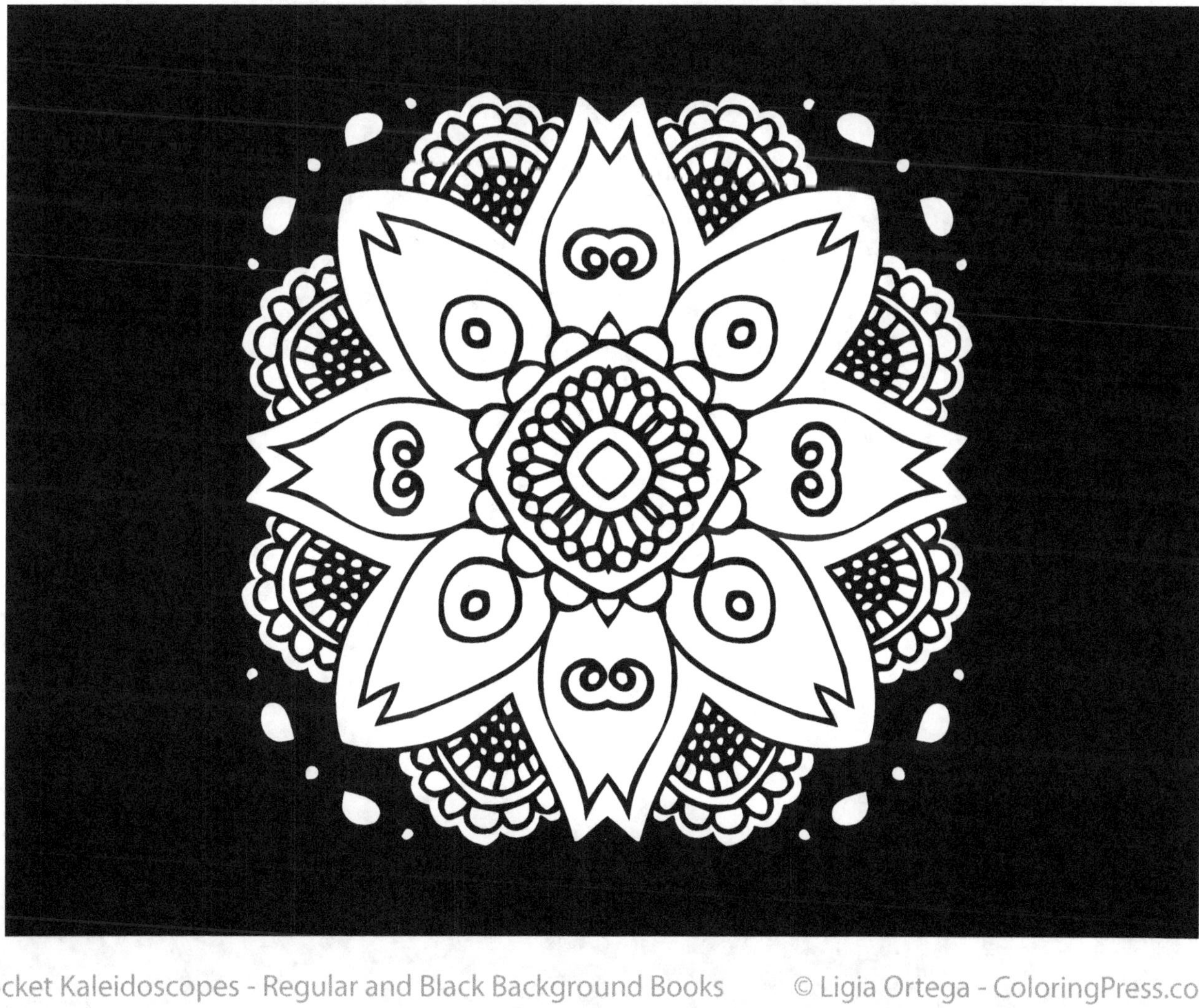

TEST & RECORD YOUR FAVORITE PALETTES & COLOR COMBINATIONS!

The Colorist Palette Reference Book works as a place to:

- keep track of your favorite color combinations
- test drive new media
- help you remember what supplies you were using if you have to pack them up /put them away before you finish coloring a page
- test and practice new techniques before you work on a coloring page
- experiment with new palettes to see if the colors play together nicely
- keep track of colors you used on a coloring page

The book has 48 full size pages in 12 different designs.
There is a small simple picture on the top half of each page and the bottom has space for swatches and lines for recording color and/or media that you used, or to take notes or keep track of blending.
The image does not have to be colored fully, it's there to see how the colors go together or for you to try new techniques. There is blank space too for notes about which coloring page you used the particular palette, media, or technique on.
This book came out of my own needs as a colorist, so I hope it will be useful! This book does not have colored pages, they are blank so you can record your own favorite palettes, combinations, or notes.

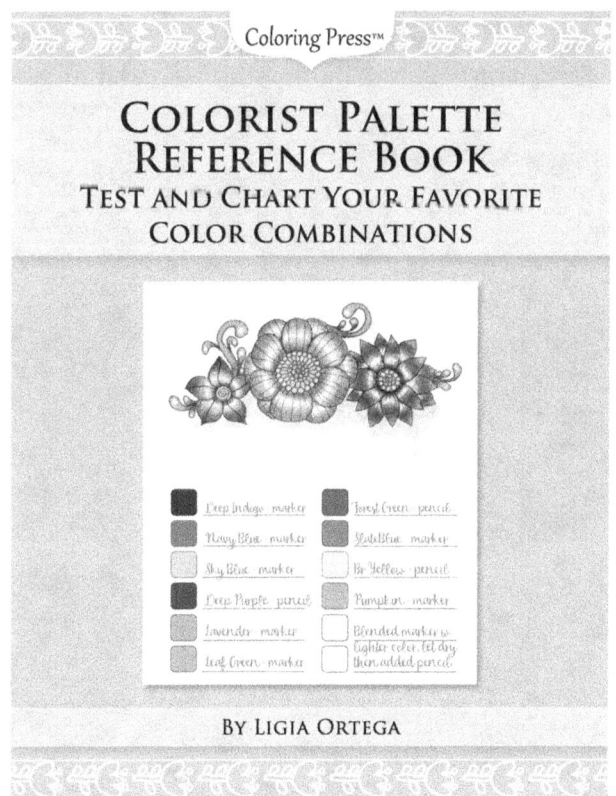

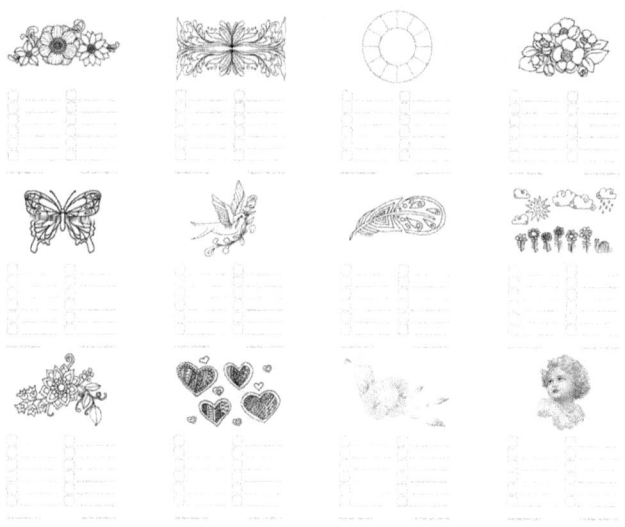

The 12 designs in the book

I hope you enjoyed Warwick Goble's Fairy Tales!

Please take a moment to leave a review on the book's Amazon page.

To find other volumes of Vintage Grayscale Adult Coloring Books, for grayscale coloring tips, to share your colored pages on Facebook, and to find my other adult coloring books, please visit:

ColoringPress.com

www.ingramcontent.com/pod-product-compliance
Lightning Source LLC
Chambersburg PA
CBHW082347220526
45470CB00008B/2673